... Trainee Book

The CELTA

Certificate in Teaching English to Speakers of Other Languages

Course

Second Edition

Peter Watkins

Scott Thornbury

Sandy Millin

CAMBRIDGE

Shaftesbury Road, Cambridge CB2 8EA, United Kingdom

One Liberty Plaza, 20th Floor, New York, NY 10006, USA

477 Williamstown Road, Port Melbourne, VIC 3207, Australia

314–321, 3rd Floor, Plot 3, Splendor Forum, Jasola District Centre, New Delhi – 110025, India

103 Penang Road, #05–06/07, Visioncrest Commercial, Singapore 238467

Cambridge University Press & Assessment is a department of the University of Cambridge.

We share the University's mission to contribute to society through the pursuit of education, learning and research at the highest international levels of excellence.

www.cambridge.org
Information on this title: www.cambridge.org/9781009095341

© Cambridge University Press & Assessment 2022

First published 2022

20 19 18 17 16 15 14 13 12 11 10 9 8 7 6 5 4

Printed in Great Britain by Ashford Colour Ltd.

A catalogue record for this publication is available from the British Library

ISBN 978-1-009-09534-1 Trainee Book Paperback
ISBN 978-1-009-37220-6 Trainee Book eBook
ISBN 978-1-009-09539-6 Trainer's Manual Paperback
ISBN 978-1-009-37221-3 Trainer's Manual eBook

Contents

Introduction

What is CELTA?

The Certificate in Teaching English to Speakers of Other Languages (CELTA) is an introductory language teaching course for candidates who have little or no previous English language teaching experience. It may also be suitable for candidates with some experience but little previous training. The qualification is awarded by Cambridge English, part of the University of Cambridge.

Candidates can take CELTA full time (typically four to five weeks), or part time (from a few months to up to a year). They can take it on a face-to-face basis, online, or a mixed-mode combination of both of these formats.

There are five main topics of learning:

1 Learners and teachers, and the teaching and learning context
2 Language analysis and awareness
3 Language skills: listening, reading, speaking and writing
4 Planning and resources for different teaching contexts
5 Developing teaching skills and professionalism

CELTA is awarded to candidates who have completed the course and who have met the assessment criteria for all written and practical assignments.

The overall assessment aims for each topic are that candidates should be able to:

1   assess learner needs, and plan and teach lessons which take account of learners' backgrounds, learning preferences and current needs
2   demonstrate language knowledge and awareness, and appropriate teaching strategies
3   demonstrate knowledge about language skills and how they may be acquired
4   plan and prepare lessons designed to develop their learners' overall language competence
5   demonstrate an appropriate range of teaching skills at this level and show professional awareness and responsibility

There are two components to the assessment of CELTA:

Component One: Planning and teaching

Component Two: Classroom-related written assignments (of which there are four in total)

CELTA is internally assessed and externally moderated by a Cambridge English approved assessor, who samples portfolios and teaching practice, and who discusses and agrees the grades for all candidates.

Each CELTA programme is designed by the individual centre, using the syllabus and course objectives. Courses will have a minimum of 120 contact hours, including:

- input
- supervised lesson planning
- teaching practice (six assessed hours)
- feedback on teaching
- peer observation
- observation of experienced teachers (minimum six hours)
- consultation time

Trainees are also expected to complete a minimum of 80 additional hours' work, including pre-course preparation, reading, research, assignment writing, lesson preparation and record keeping.

For more information about CELTA, visit the Cambridge English website:

https://www.cambridgeenglish.org/teaching-english/teaching-qualifications/

The CELTA syllabus can be accessed at:

https://www.cambridgeenglish.org/images/21816-celta-syllabus.pdf

What is *The CELTA Course?*

The CELTA Course is a coursebook designed to support trainees, trainers and centres running CELTA courses. It includes both a Trainee Book and a Trainer's Manual. It is designed to be used during course input sessions (although some tasks may be set in advance of sessions or as follow-up to sessions). The bulk of the course consists of 40 units, and they are grouped under the five main topics of the course (see above).

Each unit comprises a number of tasks, starting with a warm-up task and concluding with a reflection task. From these units and tasks, course trainers will select only those elements that meet the needs and syllabus specifications of their particular courses: it is not expected that trainees will do all the units and all the tasks in the book, nor that they will do the units in the order that they occur in the book. Many of the units contain material reproduced from ELT coursebooks. The full list of that material is on pages 227–228.

As well as the units, there is extensive supplementary material, including advice on how to get the most out of teaching practice, a bank of classroom observation tasks, and a resource file that includes a glossary and recommendations for further reading.

The CELTA Course is not only a coursebook: it also serves as an invaluable resource for post-course review and reflection. We hope that it enriches your experience of CELTA, and that CELTA, in turn, opens the doorway to a fulfilling and worthwhile career in English language teaching.

1 Learning and teaching contexts

A Warm-up

1 Think back to a language learning situation you know well. Picture as many details as you can. Consider these questions:

- How many learners were in the class?
- Was it a face-to-face class or were lessons online?
- What resources were available to the teacher?
- What was the age range of the learners?
- Did the learners share a common first language (L1)?
- What reasons did the learners have for learning the language? How motivated to learn did they appear?

2 Describe the learning context you thought about to a partner. How similar are the two contexts? How do you think each context impacted on the style of teaching and the lessons generally?

> Recognizing the complex and diverse nature of ELT classrooms around the world … is the starting point of our exploration of roles, relationships and interactions in second language classrooms.
>
> Graham Hall, 2011

B Learners' purposes

1 Here are some commonly used abbreviations to describe learners' different purposes for learning English, and also the situations in which they learn and use English. Can you match them to the definitions?

1	**EFL** English as a foreign language	a	The use of a language other than the learners' L1 to teach a school subject such as science or physical education, with the aim of developing competence in both the target language and specified subject.
2	**ESL** English as a second language	b	The way in which English is now used by many non-native speakers to communicate with other non-native speakers; also called English as a lingua franca (ELF).
3	**CLIL** Content and language integrated learning	c	The teaching of English with the aim of developing a learner's ability to function effectively in a particular domain, such as business or medicine.
4	**EIL** English as an international language	d	The learning of English in a context where English is not generally the medium of communication. For example, this would include a Spanish student having English classes in Spain.
5	**ESP** English for specific purposes	e	An example of ESP with the aim of developing a learner's ability to function effectively in academic contexts, such as studying at an English medium university.
6	**EAP** English for academic purposes	f	The learning of English over a sustained period in a context where English is generally the medium of communication. For example, this would include someone from China living and working in the UK.

2 Here are profiles of learners of English. In each case, identify their purpose for learning English. Use the abbreviations above.

- Han is currently studying a course which focuses on writing essays, giving presentations and following recordings of lectures. She hopes to enrol at an English-speaking university, if she can pass the English language test required.
- Lucia is an Italian-speaking teenager who is studying English as one of her school subjects in Bologna. She also attends an English class twice a week in a local language school.
- Kazankiran is an asylum-seeker in Canada. She speaks Kurdish and Arabic, and is attending English classes with a view to settling in Canada permanently.
- Carmen, who is Brazilian, is the head of marketing in a large export company. She attends a one-to-one English class in Sao Paulo to help her in her business dealings, which are mainly with Middle Eastern clients.
- Kah-Yee is Malaysian and when she was at school, she learned mathematics in English. Her English lessons aimed to ensure that she could follow the mathematics lessons effectively.

C Needs and needs analyses

1 Which of the five learners above are likely to have the most clearly specified needs?

2 Think about the questions below. When you are ready, discuss your ideas in small groups.

a How might the needs of an ESL learner vary from those of an EFL learner?
b How might the needs of an EAP learner vary from those of an EFL learner?
c In a CLIL context, where science is being taught through the medium of English, what sort of language content would you expect to be included?
d Can you think of any implications for teaching if a student is, or will be, a user of EIL (as opposed to using English in an environment in which English is the main language)?

3 How could you find out more about the needs of a particular learner or group of learners? What questions would you ask?

Work with a partner to write some questions which you could ask a member of your TP class.

When you are ready, compare your ideas with another group.

D More differences

1 Read the quote from Graham Hall (above). As well as the learners' purpose for learning English, what other things might contribute to 'the diverse nature of ELT classrooms'?

2 Your trainer will allocate you either a), b) or c) below. Think about the needs of the learners, their likely motivations and any specific activity types that you think would, or would not, be appropriate.

a What are the similarities and differences between teaching:
- a group of 17–18-year-olds who are at B2 level of English and have just started an ESP course in business English?
- a senior manager of a local company on a 1:1 basis, who will shortly be travelling to the USA for a series of meetings?

   b What are the similarities and differences between teaching:
- a group of 40 14-year-olds who share the same language, at a secondary school in a country where English is not spoken as a first language?
- a group of 15 14-year-olds of mixed nationality, studying a three-week course in the UK over the summer?

   c What are the similarities and differences between teaching:
- an online general English class with 15 learners?
- an online general English class with one learner?

KEY WORDS FOR TEACHERS

Check you know the meanings of these terms.
- *EFL ESL CLIL EIL ESP EAP*
- *needs analysis*

REFLECTION

Complete these sentences:
1. One reason that there is no single 'correct' way to teach is that …
2. I would like to find out about the needs of my learners because …
3. I think I would be able to teach ESP in the area of …
4. EAP learners are likely to need …
5. If I had a very small class, I would try to …
6. If I had a very big class, I would try to …
7. In a class where everyone shares the same language, I would …
8. In a class where a variety of languages are spoken, I would …

Reference

Hall, G. (2011). *Exploring English Language Teaching: Language in Action*. Abingdon: Routledge, p.4.

2 Learners as individuals

A Warm-up

1 Picture this scenario: You start teaching a new class and find that everybody in the class has more or less the same level of language proficiency. However, after several lessons you start to notice some quite big differences in learners' levels. Some appear to have made more progress than others.

What reasons can you think of for these differences emerging?

2 The following learners all study in the same Beginners (A1) English class. How might their language backgrounds impact on their progress?

Name	Nationality	Languages spoken
Zhao	Chinese	Mandarin
Safia	Algerian	Derija (her local variety of Arabic), Modern standard Arabic and a little French from when she was at school
Sophie	French	French, German (from school) and Italian

B Learner Preferences

1 Think back to a language learning experience of your own. What things did you like doing? Were there any things that you did not like doing?

Look at the statements in the questionnaire and say the extent to which you agree or disagree with them, based on your experience.

2 Compare your preferences with other people. Did you have exactly the same responses as your partners? What can you learn from this about planning and teaching lessons?

---

1. I like talking in groups about things that interest us.

   disagree   1   2   3   4   5   agree

2. I like studying grammar rules on my own.

   disagree   1   2   3   4   5   agree

3. I like it when the teacher explains grammar rules.

   disagree   1   2   3   4   5   agree

4. I like having my mistakes corrected.

   disagree   1   2   3   4   5   agree

5. I like translating sentences from my language into English.

   disagree   1   2   3   4   5   agree

6. I find it useful to review lessons when I get home.

   disagree   1   2   3   4   5   agree

7. I find language learning apps useful for reviewing new words.

   disagree   1   2   3   4   5   agree

8. I like playing games in class.

   disagree   1   2   3   4   5   agree

C Motivation

1 Think back to a learning experience of your own. Which factors drove you to make an effort? Was there anything that decreased your desire to learn?

2 Pick four items from the list below that you think are most important for promoting and maintaining motivation in a language classroom. Be ready to justify your choices.

- a favourable attitude to the target language culture and its speakers
- immediate opportunities to use the language outside class
- having a good rapport with classmates
- doing well in class and a feeling of progress
- using interesting materials/books in class
- knowing there will be regular tests and examinations
- the personality of the teacher
- liking the teacher's way of teaching
- having a specific long-term goal, e.g. work, study, travel

3 When you are ready, share your list with a partner. Look at your combined list of items and try to reduce it to four.

D Language learning strategies

1 Look at the difficulties (on the left) that these learners have with their English and in learning English. Can you think of any advice to help them?

2 Match the difficulty on the left with the most appropriate strategy used to compensate for it on the right.

Learner A

I get very nervous and anxious in English lessons …

1

… so I watch videos on the internet with subtitles.

Learner B

We learn a lot of new words but I often forget most of them …

2

… so I find information about topics and plan what I can say.

Learner C

I worry when I have to speak English in social situations …

3

… so I do some deep breathing exercises before I go to class.

Learner D

Listening is really difficult for me – people speak too fast!

4

… so I arrive early to class and talk to the teacher before class starts.

Learner E

I don't get to practise speaking very much …

5

… so I got an app on my phone and I make flash cards, which I look at a few times a week.

3 Which learner(s) …

   i … decided they needed to control their emotions?

   ii … decided they needed more social interaction?

   iii … realized that their learning wasn't working very well?

4 What advice would you give these learners?

   a I need to improve my grammar – what can I do?

   b I want to improve my vocabulary – what can I do?

   c I want to improve my speaking – what can I do?

> Simply stated, language learning strategies … are purposeful mental actions … used by a learner to regulate his or her second or foreign language learning.
>
> Rebecca Oxford, 2018

E Learner training

Learner training refers to the training given to learners to help them use strategies to become more effective in their learning and to be able to make the most of learning opportunities, both inside and outside the classroom.

1 Look at the coursebook you are using for TP. Does it provide any learner training? For example, is there a section in each unit that gives learning advice, or are there any questionnaires or other forms of guidance at the beginning of the book? If so, does the material present individual strategies, or several strategies together that share the same goal?

2 Look at the activities you will use in your next teaching practice lesson.

   i Are there any opportunities to give advice to your learners on how to maximize their learning?

   ii Which strategies do you think would help your class the most?

   iii How could you present the strategies?

KEY WORDS FOR TEACHERS

Check you know the meanings of these terms.
- *learning strategies*
- *learner training*
- *learner autonomy*
- *learner preferences*

REFLECTION

Answer the questions.

1 From what you already know about the learners you are teaching, how similar or different are they, with regards to the things we have discussed in this unit?
2 What other individual factors might contribute to diversity in the classroom?
3 What practical things can a teacher do to make everyone feel equally valued and included in lessons?
4 Look at the quote from Bonny Norton. What are the advantages of teachers 'understanding the histories and lived experiences' of their learners? How might they attempt to do this?

> It is only by understanding the histories and lived experiences of language learners that the language teacher can create conditions that will facilitate social interaction both in the classroom and in the wider community, and help learners claim the right to speak.
>
> Bonny Norton, 2013

References

Norton, B. (2013). *Identity and Language Learning: Extending the Conversation* (2nd edition). Bristol: Multilingual Matters, p.179.

Oxford, R. (2018). Language Learning Strategies. In A. Burns and J.C. Richards (eds.), *The Cambridge Guide to Learning English as a Second Language*. Cambridge: Cambridge University Press p.81.

3 What do teachers do?

A Warm-up

1 Who am I?

Listen to the clues that your trainer gives you. Can you guess what profession is being described?

2 What clues could you use to describe the work of a language teacher?

B Roles of teachers

1 Match what the teacher says on the left with their purpose for saying it, on the right.

1	I can see how much effort you put into your homework! That's great because you really are improving.	a	to correct learner output
2	When I was listening to you in your groups, I heard someone say: 'Can you to swim?'. How can we make the English better?	b	to give instructions
3	Work with your partner and write five sentences.	c	to motivate and encourage
4	Hi, Jorge – did you have a good weekend?	d	to check understanding of new language
5	Look at this example: I used to live in Athens. Notice I don't live there now – it's finished, completed.	e	to build rapport in the class
6	So, if you do something on the spur of the moment, do you plan it first? Do you think a lot?	f	to focus on language

2 Look at the examples of teacher talk on the next page.
  i   Which two are eliciting language from learners?
  ii Which one is building rapport?
  iii Which one is checking an exercise?
  iv Which two are part of managing the class?

A After a modal verb – things like *will, may, might* – what sort of word do we need?

B OK, stop talking to your partners now. Thanks. Monika – tell us about your group. What ideas did you discuss?

C Alex, please stop talking now. Alex. Thank you. Listen to what Monika is saying.

[As learners come into the room]

D Hello, Wang, how are you? Did you watch the football last night? What a game!

E Good. Yes, the answer for question 3 is B. Good. And question 4? What's the answer for question 4?

F What phrase can we use when we want someone to repeat something?

When you are ready, compare your ideas with a partner.

C Observation

1 Watch the lesson and complete Observation Task 14 on page 198.

2 Compare your notes with a partner.

3 Look back at the questions that were asked. Which questions were 'real' questions (i.e. the teacher did not already know the answer) and which ones were 'display' questions (i.e. the teacher invites the learners to display their knowledge about language)?

D Anticipating roles

A new teacher gets the following instruction:

> Use the grammar presentation on *used to + infinitive* on page 57 of the coursebook. Do the gap-fill exercise that follows, but also add another more communicative activity to practise the new language. Perhaps the learners could talk in groups about their childhoods, for example.

- What will the teacher need to do before the lesson?
- What roles will the teacher almost certainly need to fulfil during the lesson, or what things will they need to do?
- Can you anticipate any other roles that the teacher may need to fulfil, or what things they will need to do?

KEY WORDS FOR TEACHERS

Check you know the meanings of these terms.

- *real question*
- *display question*
- *rapport*
- *eliciting*
- *checking understanding*
- *monitoring*

REFLECTION

1 How do the roles of a language teacher (or things they do) compare with those of:
   - a maths teacher?
   - a tour guide?
2 Think back to a language learning experience of your own. Which teacher roles did you feel were most important? Why?
3 Look back at the observation sheet. Which things:
   - have you already performed when teaching?
   - have you performed in some other work role or as a student?
   - are you confident of performing?
   - do you think will take a lot of practice?
   - do you think can be made easier by planning what you will say or do during the lesson?
4 What roles will you need to perform in your next TP lesson?

4 Introduction to analysing language

A Warm-up

1 Imagine language as a pyramid, with its features in descending order from the smallest features to the largest. Map these aspects of language onto the pyramid:

phrases   *sentences*   *sounds*   *syllables*   *texts*   *words*

2 Can you think of other features of language that could go onto the pyramid?

> The answer to the question 'What do I teach when I teach English?' is, of course, 'language'. As we have been saying all along – if you're a language teacher, language should be your thing!
>
> Tim Marr and Fiona English, 2019

B Basic concepts and terminology

1 Match the terms (1–10) with their definitions (a–j). For example: 10–h.

Terms used to talk aboutlanguage	Definitions
1 vocabulary	a the rules that govern the way words are combined, adapted and sequenced in order to form sentences
2 grammar	b the purpose for which a language item is used, e.g. making requests; predicting
3 structure	c the place (in a text, or in the physical world) where an instance of language occurs
4 concept	d the way that language sounds when it is spoken

5 function	e the area of language learning that is concerned with word knowledge
6 register	f a continuous piece of speech or writing, having a communicative purpose and a distinctive organization
7 pronunciation	g a pattern that generates examples, such as the present perfect: *I've seen …; she's met …; they've worked …*
8 context	h the way that words or sequences of words are spoken or written, e.g. /miːt/ is written as *meat* or *meet*; the past of *meet* is *met*
9 text	i the way that spoken or written language is adapted to its particular situation of use, such as its degree of formality, e.g. *Please remain seated* v *Sit down!*
10 form	j the basic meaning of a word or grammar pattern, e.g. *You can go now* means *You are free to go now.*

2 Read the following short text and identify:

a what type of text it is
b the context in which it is typically found
c its function
d its register
e any sets of words that relate to the topic of the text
f any distinctive features of its grammar

> For the perfect cup, use one teabag per person and add freshly drawn boiling water.
> Leave standing for 3–5 minutes before stirring gently.
> Can be served with or without milk and sugar.

3 What is the effect on meaning of making the following changes to the above text?

1 For the perfect cup → For a perfect cup
e.g. 'the perfect cup' suggests we know which perfect cup – perhaps because there is only one; this can have a significant effect on meaning, as in 'The dog bit me' v 'A dog bit me'.
2 use one teabag → use one bag of tea: Can you think of other examples that follow the same pattern?
3 add freshly drawn boiling water → add boiling water: What kind of effect is the writer trying to create?
4 boiling water → boiled water: Finished or unfinished?
5 Leave standing → Leave to stand: The same or different?
6 Can be served → It can be served: Why is 'it' not necessary in this text?
7 Can be served → Should be served: Which one suggests more choice?

Syllabus decisions

For teaching purposes, the different aspects of language are often separated out and organized into a sequence to form a syllabus. Here, for example, are the first two units of an intermediate level course:

	Learning objectives	Grammar	Vocabulary	Pronunciation
Unit 1 **And we're off!**	▪ Talk about personal achievements ▪ Discuss good employee qualities ▪ Make and respond to introductions ▪ Write a comment on a blog post ▪ Practice a job interview	▪ Tense review (simple and continuous) ▪ Dynamic and stative verbs	▪ Describing accomplishments ▪ Describing key qualities	▪ Saying the letter *y*
Unit 2 **The future of food**	▪ Talk about trends ▪ Talk about preparing food ▪ Make offers in social situations ▪ Write the results of a survey ▪ Create a plan to improve a restaurant	▪ Real conditionals ▪ Clauses with *after, until, when*	▪ Describing trends ▪ Preparing food	▪ Saying the vowel sounds /aɪ/, /i/, and /eɪ/ ▪ Listening for deleted /t/ sounds

Functional language	Listening	Reading	Writing	Speaking
▪ Meet someone you don't know; introduce someone to others **Real-world strategy** ▪ Respond to an introduction		**Flipping your job interview** ▪ An article on interview skills	**A comment** ▪ A comment on an article ▪ Agreeing and disagreeing	▪ Talk about a new activity ▪ Talk about personal achievements ▪ Describe your personal qualities ▪ Play an introduction game **Time to speak** ▪ Ask and answer interview questions
▪ Make, accept, and refuse offers in social situations **Real-world strategy** ▪ Acknowledge an acceptance	**Cool food** ▪ A conversation between friends		**A report** ▪ The results of a survey about eating habits ▪ Reporting research results	▪ Talk about fusion foods ▪ Discuss ideas to avoid food waste ▪ Explain a favorite recipe ▪ Offer food and drink to others **Time to speak** ▪ Present a restaurant rescue plan

Evolve Level 4

1 Work in pairs. Here are some more items from the same coursebook syllabus. Decide which column they go into: Grammar, Vocabulary, Pronunciation, or Functional language.

- present and past passive
- make an apology and explain what happened
- saying /s/ or /z/ at the end of a word
- reported questions
- talking about time and money
- *was / were going to*
- stressing long words
- keep your listener engaged
- *I wish*
- saying long or short vowel sounds

2 Work in pairs. What factors might determine the choice of items to put into a syllabus?

D Parts of speech

In English there are at least eight parts of speech (also called word classes). These are:

- **nouns**, such as *cup, teabag, minutes*
- **pronouns**, i.e. words that take the place of nouns, such as *it, they, ours*
- **verbs**, such as *use, be, leave, stirring*
- **adjectives**, such as *perfect, boiling*
- **adverbs**, such as *freshly, gently*

- *prepositions*, such as *for, with, without*
- *determiners*, such as the definite article *the*, the indefinite article *a/an*, and words like *one, some, this*, when they go in front of nouns, as *one teabag*
- *conjunctions*, i.e. words that join parts of sentences, such as *and, or, that*

Many common words can function as different parts of speech, depending on their context. *Water*, for example, can be a noun (*a cup of water*) or a verb (*water the garden*). *One* can be a determiner (*one teabag*) or a pronoun (*would you like one?*)

Work in pairs. Identify the part of speech of each word in this text.

> *In the empty doorway many petals are scattered;*
> *As they fall they blend with the song of the birds.*
> *Slowly, the bright spring sun appears in the window*
> *And a thin line of smoke drifts from the incense burner.*

John Stevens, 1977

In	the	empty	doorway	many	petals	are	scattered
preposition	determiner	adjective					

As	they	fall	they	blend	with	the	song	of	the	birds
conjunction	pronoun									

Slowly	the	bright	spring	sun	appears	in	the	window
			noun					

And	a	thin	line	of	smoke	drifts	from	the	incense	burner

E Content words v grammar words

Unlike some languages, English doesn't have a lot of grammar in the form of verb endings (as in Russian) or noun cases (as in German). Instead, a lot of grammatical meaning is carried by the 'grammar' words. These act as the 'glue' that connects the 'content' words, i.e. those words that carry the main meaning.

1 Work in pairs. Look at the poem from the last activity.

　1 Identify the content words. These are typically nouns, adjectives, verbs and adverbs. The first line has been done for you: the content words are underlined.

　　In the <u>empty</u> <u>doorway</u> many <u>petals</u> are <u>scattered</u>;
　　As they fall they blend with the song of the birds.
　　Slowly, the bright spring sun appears in the window
　　And a thin line of smoke drifts from the incense burner.

　2 What is the proportion of content words to grammar words? (There are 39 words altogether).

　3 Do you think this would be the same for most texts? Choose a text at random and check.

2 What do you notice about the grammar words? Here are some clues to help you: frequency, length, repetition, stress, novelty.

3 A very important sub-group of grammar words are auxiliary verbs (sometimes called 'helping verbs').

Look at this summary – from a coursebook – of the main uses of auxiliary verbs:

1.2 Uses of auxiliaries (1): auxiliaries in verb forms 1B **4** p11

- We make continuous verb forms with *be* + verb+*ing*:
  *I'm **doing** a Master's.* (Present Continuous) *She **was hoping** to do her first degree in four years.* (Past Continuous)

- We make perfect verb forms with *have* + past participle:
  *It's something I**'ve** (= have) **wanted** to do for ages.*
  (Present Perfect Simple)

- We make all passive verb forms with *be* + past participle:
  *I **was told** you were really enjoying it.* (Past Simple Passive)

- In the Present Simple and Past Simple we use a form of *do* to make questions and negatives: ***Does** she **know** this guy?*
  *I **didn't think** you were coming.*

MODAL VERBS

- We also use modal verbs as auxiliaries. The modal verbs are:
  will, would, can, could, may, might, shall, should, ought to, must and *have to*.

- Modal verbs are different from the auxiliaries *be*, *do* and *have* because they have their own meanings. Most modal verbs also have more than one meaning:
  *I**'ll** see you at six.* (a promise)
  *I think we**'ll** win.* (a prediction)
  ***Can** you pick me up?* (a request)
  *He **can** play the piano.* (ability)
  *You **must** be here at nine.* (obligation)
  *You **must** see that film.* (strong recommendation)

---

face2face Upper Intermediate

Work in pairs or small groups.

a Think of the learners you are teaching now. Rate this explanation in terms of its clarity, economy and usefulness, from those learners' point of view.

b Assuming this is a review, at what stages in the learners' progress would they have likely met these points for the first time? (You might want to check with the coursebook you are currently using.)

c Can you think of any other uses of auxiliaries not mentioned here?

KEY WORDS FOR TEACHERS

Check you know the meanings of these terms.

- *form, concept*
- *structure, function, register*
- *phrase*
- *part of speech (or word class)*
- *syllable*
- *noun, verb, adjective, adverb, determiner, article, pronoun, preposition, conjunction*
- *content words, grammar words*
- *auxiliary verbs*
- *modal verbs*
- *text*

REFLECTION

This unit has introduced you to some key elements of language analysis – and a lot of terminology! Reflect on your language analysis skills at this point in time:

1 How would you rate yourself, on a scale of 1 to 10, in terms of the following?
   1 Your current understanding of the main concepts introduced in this unit.
   2 Your grasp of the terminology that has been used.
   3 Your familiarity with the resources available for self-development in this area.
   4 Your motivation to improve your language analysis skills.
2 Can you identify any specific language areas on which you would appreciate more clarification right now?

Reference

Marr, T. and English, F. (2019). *Rethinking TESOL in Diverse Global Settings*. London: Bloomsbury Academic, p.230.

Ryokan, trans. Stevens, J. (1977). *One Robe, One Bowl: The Zen Poetry of Ryokan*. New York: Weatherhill, p.37.

5 Introduction to researching language

A Warm-up

Work in pairs. Answer the questions.

1 In the box are some questions which a teacher might need the answers to before working on grammar, vocabulary or functional language with learners. Look at the language analysis form from your trainer. Which questions do you need to answer to complete the form?

> a What situations is the language item likely to be used in?
> b What does the language mean (in this context)?
> c What is the written form of the language? (What does it look like?)
> d What is the pronunciation (spoken form) of the language? (What does it sound like?)
> e What problems might learners have with the meaning or use of the language?
> f What problems might learners have with the written form of the language?
> g What problems might learners have with the pronunciation of the language?

2 What sources could a teacher use to find out this information?

B Researching language using coursebooks

1 Your TP tutor has given you a grammar lesson to teach on the topic of 'modals of obligation'. Look at the coursebook extract and complete the following tasks.

   i Underline the words and phrases which express obligation and advice.

   ii Work with a partner. Work out the rules from the example sentences.

The words or phrases you have identified form part of 'model sentences'. You can use them as your examples when working on grammar with learners.

CULTURE SHOCK

Some people choose to live in another country, other people have to move for family or work reasons. If you're going to live in a new place for some time, you ought to be prepared to experience culture shock at some point.

At first, when you're in a very different environment, everything seems exciting and new. Then, the differences start to be annoying. Life feels too fast or too slow, the food tastes strange, you miss your favourite television programmes. Laws are different – there are things you mustn't do here that you can do at home. This is culture shock.

The good news is, you don't have to spoil your experience of living abroad. Culture shock doesn't usually last very long.

Empower B1+

2 The next activity in the book asks learners to identify the meaning of four modals of obligation from the context, plus four extra modals of obligation. Try it yourself:

> e Complete rules 1–5 with the words in the box.
>
> can   can't   don't have to   have to
> must   mustn't   ought to   should
>
> 1 We use _____ and _____ to give advice.
> 2 We use _____ to say that something is not necessary.
> 3 We use _____ and _____ to say that something is necessary.
> 4 We use _____ and _____ when we say that something is forbidden/not allowed.
> 5 We use _____ to talk about a choice to do something.

Empower B1+

3 At the back of the coursebook, you can often find a summary of the grammar, along with some extra information. Use the grammar summary on the next page to complete as much of this table as you can.

Verb	Use	Notes / Possible problems
must	when we make the rules	no past or future form – use *have to* instead questions with *must* are very rare
have to		
have got to		
mustn't		[no information in the summary]
can't		[no information in the summary]
couldn't		[no information in the summary]
don't have to		[no information in the summary]
should		
ought to		

6A Modals of obligation

 must and **have to**

We use *must* when we make the rules:
*I **must get** a good night's sleep tonight.*
We use *have to* when we talk about other people's rules:
*You **have to buy** a ticket before you get on the train.*
There is no past or future form of *must*. When we talk about rules in the past or future, we always use the correct form of *have to*:
*When you go to India, you**'ll have to** get a visa.*
*I **had to** wear a uniform at school.*

> **Tip**
> Don't use contractions with *have to*:
> *I have to go.* NOT ~~I've to go.~~

> **Tip**
> * Often there is not much difference in meaning between *must* or *have to*. *Have to* is much more common than *must*, especially in spoken English.
> * *have got to* is also used in spoken English and means the same as *have to*.
> * Questions with *must* are very rare.

 mustn't, **can't** and **don't have to**

We use *mustn't* or *can't* to say that something is not allowed. We often use *mustn't* when we make the rules and *can't* to talk about other people's rules:
*I **mustn't** forget to email my mum.*
*We **can't** cross the road yet – the light's still red.*
For things which were not allowed in the past, use *couldn't*:
*I **couldn't** work in India because I only had a tourist visa.*

We use *don't have to* when there is no obligation. It means it's not necessary to do something:
*University students **don't have to wear** a uniform.*
*I **didn't have to** call a taxi. Robert drove me home.*

 **should** and **ought to**

We use *should* or *ought to* to give advice and recommendations. They have the same meaning, but *should* is much more common:
*We **should see** as much as possible. We **shouldn't waste** time.*
*We **ought to see** as much as possible. We **ought not to waste** time.*

Empower B1+

C Researching language using teacher's books

This is an excerpt from the teacher's book which corresponds to the student's book pages we looked at in task B:

 CAREFUL!

Students are likely to make a number of errors of form and use with modals of obligation.

Problems with form include using the wrong verb form after a modal, e.g. ~~I must to go~~ (Correct form = *I must **go***). With *have to*, students may also contract the structure inappropriately, e.g. ~~I've to go to the doctor~~ (Correct form = *I have **to go** …*). They also make mistakes with word order, e.g. ~~We have also to wear a uniform~~ (Correct form = *We **also have to wear**…*).

The difference between *mustn't* and *don't have to* can also be difficult for students at this level, e.g. ~~You don't have to eat too many sweets~~. *They're bad for you.* (Correct form = ***You mustn't eat** …*), and ~~I mustn't go to the shops~~. *There's enough milk* (Correct form = *I **don't have to** go …*).

Empower B1+ TB

Use the information in the excerpt to answer the questions.

1 What is the correct verb form after a modal like *must* or *can*? What is one problem which learners might have with the form?
2 What two other problems with the form of modals of obligation might learners have?
3 What problem with the meaning of *mustn't* and *don't have to* might learners have? Why? You may wish to look back at B3 to help you.

D Researching language using reference books

A reputable grammar book aimed at teachers will generally focus on key areas which it is useful for teachers to work on with learners, including potential problems which learners might have.

Your trainer will give you a relevant excerpt from a grammar reference book. Speak to everybody in the group. Which of the questions from task A does each excerpt answer?

E Putting it all together

Work with a partner.

1 Look back at the questions in A. How many of them can you now answer about modals of obligation? Which sources have you used to gather this information? Which sources did you find to be more or less useful in your research?

2 In this TP, do you feel like you would be prepared to:
  * communicate the most important points connected to the grammar?
  * answer learners' questions about the grammar?

KEY WORDS FOR TEACHERS

Check you know the meanings of these terms.
* *meaning*
* *form*
* *pronunciation*
* *context*
* *model sentence*
* *modal verb*
* *auxiliary verb*
* *infinitive*

REFLECTION

To what extent do you agree with the following statements?
* You should research the language items you plan to teach before you plan how to teach them.
* You need to research quite different information when you're teaching vocabulary rather than grammar.

- The best place to find out information about grammar you're teaching is in a grammar book.
- You should have a comprehensive knowledge of new language you're planning to teach before you enter the classroom.
- It's important to teach learners everything you know about the new language item(s) you're working on.
- You should be able to answer all of the learners' questions about the language you are teaching during the lesson.
- Predicting possible problems learners might have with the language will help you to feel more confident in the classroom.

Compare your answers with a partner.

6 Vocabulary

A Warm-up

1 Work in pairs or groups. Brainstorm as many words you can think of that relate to the topic of *gardening*. You have one minute.

2 Compare your words with those of another group. Identify how many you had that were the same and how many were different.

3 Decide if it is possible to make connections between any of your words. For example, if you had *tree* and *leaf*, you could say that *a leaf is a part of a tree*; *flower* and *pot* can combine to make *flowerpot*.

B Lexical meaning

Read the following text. Identify any words that you brainstormed in A. Then answer the questions.

> **Operation Tree Salvage**
>
> To know a <u>good</u> pruning job from a <u>bad</u> one it is necessary to understand a few principles of tree <u>growth</u>. First of all, a tree, like all plants, is a <u>living organism</u>. We know that it manufactures its own food in the <u>leaves</u>. <u>Raw materials</u>, water and minerals, taken in by the <u>roots</u>, are transported up to the leaves and there, in the presence of sunlight and chlorophyll (green matter), are converted to simple food. These in turn flow back through the tree, nourishing <u>growing</u> cells throughout the plant. This intricate transportation system and a layer of active growth cells lie just beneath the <u>bark</u>. There are a number of theories on the forces that put this system into motion. However, for our purposes it is evident that the <u>foliage</u> of the tree is essential to this process. It stands to reason then that we can't just lop off all the major branches of a large tree and expect it to survive.
>
> Granted that in some cases pruning will have to be severe, but if it is done properly the tree will have a chance to live. When a large <u>branch</u> is cut off and a stub is left, the growth processes stop in the projected stub, but continue their natural course of flow at its base in the parent branch. Each year as the tree grows it rebuilds a new growth ring around the stub. This is noted as a swelling, and will continue to <u>grow</u> in size each succeeding year. In the meantime, the <u>dead</u> stub is exposed to the elements and begins to rot away. In time it will decay back to the stem or <u>trunk</u> and be sloughed off and the original wound may close over with new growth rings. Usually before this happens, the organisms causing <u>decay</u> of the stub enter the main stem and begin their slow but deadly work there, so that in time the entire tree may become <u>decadent</u>.

Pat Gallavan, 1959

1 Match the sets of words (1–5; underlined in the text) with the term that describes their relationship (a–e).

words	relationship
1 *to survive, to live; leaves, foliage; rot, decay*	a antonyms (opposite meaning)
2 *good, bad; living, dead*	b word family (words that share the same root)
3 *living organism; raw materials*	c lexical set (words that are thematically related, or that form parts of a larger unit)
4 *grow, growing, growth; decay, decadent*	d synonyms (same or similar meaning)
5 *leaves, roots, branch, bark, trunk*	e collocations (words the commonly occur together)

2 Find more examples of each category in the text.

C Word formation

In English, new words can be formed by combining old ones – a process called 'compounding', or by adding prefixes and suffixes (such as *pre-* or *–less*) – a process called 'affixation'. Some words in fact comprise more than one word: they take the form of multi-word units (also called 'chunks'). Phrasal verbs are a kind of multi-word unit composed of a verb and a particle, e.g. *down, in, over.*

1 Match the modes of formation (1–4) with the examples from the text (a–d).

1 compounding (= putting two or more words together to make one)	a *cut off, close over, rot away*
2 affixation (= adding prefixes or suffixes)	b *sunlight, meantime*
3 multi-word unit (chunk) (= two or more words that have one complete meaning)	c *organism; transportation; rebuilds*
4 phrasal verb (= verb plus particle, having one complete meaning)	d *first of all; in the meantime; in turn*

2 Phrasal verbs, such as *cut off*, are a common feature of English. They cause learners problems, both of meaning (they are often idiomatic) and form (there are constraints on the way their components can be sequenced).

Below are some examples of phrasal verbs in context (taken from the Cambridge Corpus[1]). The parts of the phrasal verbs are underlined. Use the examples to complete the table.

Phrasal verb	Idiomatic		Syntax	
	yes	no	parts are separable	parts are not separable
set off				
give back				
look after				
get on				
knock over				
make up				

In June 1990, 18 children and 48 volunteers <u>set off</u> for Trail's Edge.
And what time did you <u>set off</u>? 'At half past ten this morning.'
I <u>set off</u> at four o'clock: it took me half an hour to get through.

He felt he wanted to <u>give</u> something <u>back</u> to the Health Service.
In 1969 John Lennon <u>gave back</u> his MBE as a protest over Biafra and the Vietnam war.
Then he signed my card and <u>gave</u> it <u>back</u> to me.

Because we lived in my mother's flat, she could <u>look after</u> my baby a lot of the time.
And I also had a child, and I had to <u>look after</u> her at the time.
Of course you would have your aunty there to <u>look after</u> you.

They didn't <u>get on,</u> she and Gwen, and they had nothing in common.
How did you <u>get on</u> with the local people?
What happened was that Roger and I never <u>got on</u> really.

He reached for his glass and <u>knocked</u> it <u>over</u>.
I managed to <u>knock over</u> the bucket with the mop.
One of the boys had <u>knocked</u> a table <u>over</u> on his way to the bathroom.

They <u>made up</u> a story about some tycoon making a big cash withdrawal.
That's not actually true – I just <u>made</u> it <u>up</u>.
Any historical novelist seeking authenticity does not <u>make</u> the facts <u>up</u>.

[1]A corpus is a large database of authentic texts, both written and spoken, used for research purposes.

Vocabulary focus

1 Study these three coursebook activities. Identify the aspect of lexical meaning or word formation that each one targets.

a

Vocabulary and Speaking
make and *do*

1 a Work in pairs. Do we use *make* or *do* with these words/phrases? Then check in **VOCABULARY 6.1** p141.

the cleaning   a decision   a course   a mistake
homework   money   friends   nothing   exercise
the washing-up   a noise   the shopping   dinner
some work   the washing   a degree   an excuse
someone laugh/cry   an exam   up your mind
the housework   progress   a cake   an appointment
someone a favour   a mess of something

do the cleaning   make a decision

b Work in pairs. Take turns to test each other.

a decision   make a decision

face2face Intermediate

b

a Read about William and his change of lifestyle. What part of his life does he change?

William was working as a **legal** adviser. He was an **experienced** and **responsible** employee with **regular** working hours. But he was bored. He was not a **patient** man either and wanted to change his life before it was too late. So he handed in his notice, and explained in a **formal** and **polite** manner that he was not **satisfied** with his situation.
He then started working for himself as a gardener and discovered that it was even better than **expected**. He enjoyed working outdoors, he loved seeing all the wildlife around him, and he felt like a very **fortunate** man. He was happy that he had been **honest** with himself and followed his heart.

b Look at the adjectives in bold in the text. Add the opposite of the adjectives in the correct place in the table. Use a dictionary to help you.

un-	in-	im-
ir-	il-	dis-

Empower B2

c

WordWise

Expressions with *way*

1 **Look at these sentences from the unit so far. Complete them with the phrases from the list.**

the way | the same way | in my way
on my way | one way or another | way too

1 Twitter allows people who think _____ to get together.
2 Liam, you're _____ . I can't see the screen.
3 I was _____ to meet you when I saw a TV cameraman.
4 This is _____ difficult. I hate guessing.
5 How is Twitter changing _____ we do things?
6 I don't know how but I'm going to fix the situation _____ .

2 **Which phrase in Exercise 1 means:**

1 in a similar manner
2 very / really
3 coming
4 between me and
5 the manner or method
6 from one perspective

something else

Think B2

2 Work in pairs. Decide how you would follow up each of these activities in class.

E Lexical difficulty

1   Work in pairs. Decide which of these words in the text in B might cause learners difficulty in understanding. Give reasons.

bark   chlorophyll   lop off   parent   pruning   stub   sunlight

2   Choose up to five words in the text that you would pre-teach before giving it to a class of upper-intermediate students to read.

3   Discuss what factors determined your choice of words.

Reference

Gallavan, P. (1959). *Operation Tree Salvage*. The Green Thumb, Colorado Forestry and Horticulture Association, recovered from https://www.gutenberg.org/files/59948/59948-0.txt

7 Teaching vocabulary

Warm-up

1   Imagine you are going to travel to a country where you do not speak the language. How are you more likely to prepare?

   a by learning some words and phrases
   b by studying the grammar rules of the language

Explain your choice.

2   Look at the quote from David Wilkins. To what extent do you agree with him?

> The fact is that while without grammar very little can be conveyed, without vocabulary *nothing* can be conveyed.
>
> David Wilkins, 1972

3   Compare your answers to 2 with the other members of your group.

B Meaning, form and use

1   Your trainer will teach you a word from another language. What do you need to know about the word to be able to use it when speaking? And what about when writing?

2   What information will learners need about nearly every word or phrase they learn? What information will they sometimes need?

3   What are the implications of the above for learning and teaching?

C Presenting techniques

1   Look at the teaching techniques listed below. For each one say whether it primarily focuses on form, meaning or use.

	Teaching technique	focus on form, meaning or use
1	the teacher shows pictures, realia or uses mime	
2	the teacher uses definitions	
3	the teacher uses translation	
4	the teacher uses word relationships (e.g. *it means the opposite of …, it's a type of …, it's a part of …*)	
5	learners repeat the word or phrase	
6	the teacher writes the word or phrase on the board	
7	the teacher indicates the stress pattern on a word after writing it on the board	
8	the teacher provides additional information (e.g. *this word is very informal*)	
9	the teacher highlights the use of new vocabulary in context (e.g. by showing an authentic piece of communication, such as a video clip)	

2   Which techniques have you used in your own teaching?

3   Which techniques would you use to teach these groups of words?

Group 1 (elementary class): *grape, plum, strawberry, cherry*
Group 2 (pre-intermediate class): *to dig, to paint, to saw, to hammer*
Group 3 (intermediate class): a pet, *to put down (a pet), to vaccinate, a vet*
Group 4 (upper-intermediate class): *alone, lonely, solitude, isolated*

D Eliciting vocabulary

1   Eliciting new language can help teachers gauge and respond to their learners' knowledge in a student-centred way. Look at a–e below. Which pieces of advice do you consider to be helpful for a new teacher when eliciting? Compare your ideas with a partner.

a   Try to trick the learners or they will find it too easy.
b   Plan how you will elicit things before the lesson.
c   Ensure eliciting is as simple and quick as possible.
d   Make sure you elicit everything – never give in and just tell the learners.
e   If the learners don't get the word quickly, try giving them the first sound of the word.

2   How would you try to elicit the following words?

a   a watch
b   a game show
c   a hurricane

3 Complete this summary about eliciting new language. The first and last letters of the missing words have been given to you.

> It is good to i_____e learners when presenting new language. However, there is also nothing wrong with teachers g____g learners information sometimes. If you e____t new language, make sure it is done q_____y. Be p_____d to tell learners what something means, rather than create an elaborate g_____g game!

E Checking understanding

1 Even after a focus on meaning, teachers sometimes need to check that learners have understood. Look at the following techniques. Talk to a partner about the strengths and weaknesses of each.

   a The teacher asks a learner to translate the word (or phrase) into their own language.
   b The teacher monitors how words are used in a subsequent activity.
   c The teacher asks, 'Do you understand?'.
   d The teacher asks the students to use the word in a sentence.
   e The teacher asks short, easy-to-answer questions. For example: 'If you are *furious*, are you a little bit angry, or very angry?'.

2 A teacher has just taught the word *shoplift*, and given the example sentence 'The kids were caught shoplifting sweets.'.

   She then asks:
   a Did the kids pay for the sweets?
   b Is this a crime?

   Work with a partner and discuss the following questions.
   i Why does the teacher ask these questions?
   ii Answer questions a and b.
   iii What do you notice about the answers?

3 Imagine you are teaching the words and phrases in bold in the following sentences. What questions would you ask to clarify understanding?

   1 She picked up her **briefcase** and left.
      (The teacher is worried that the word will be confused with 'suitcase'.)
   2 The car was **a write-off** after the accident.
      (The teacher is concerned that learners will not understand the scale of the damage.)
   3 Houses are often more expensive near the **coast**.
      (The teacher is concerned that the word will be confused with 'border'.)

4 Work in a small group. Discuss when you think it is useful to use questions such as those in 2 and 3 above, and when you think it is not useful. Be ready to report your ideas back to the class.

F Practising techniques

1 A teacher has just presented a set of vocabulary relating to transport. Here are some practice activities. Do you think they are all useful? What are the differences between them? Share your ideas with your group.

---

1 The learners discuss transport problems and developments in their own countries.
2 Learners work in small groups. The teacher gives each group a set of cards with one of the target words written on each card. One learner must take a card and can use mime, drawings, definitions, relationships with other words, or any other means to elicit the word from the other members of her group.
3 The teacher prepares a gap-fill exercise and the learners have to complete the gaps with one of the target words. For example: 'When the _____ _____ turns red, you have to stop!' (Answer: traffic light).
4 The learners work in pairs to write a short dialogue, in which they have to use a minimum of four of the new words and phrases.
5 At the beginning of the following lesson, the teacher re-elicits the words and phrases taught.

---

2 Look back at the groups of words in C3 (above). How would you practise them with learners?

KEY WORDS FOR TEACHERS

Check you know the meanings of these terms.

- *eliciting*
- *form, meaning, use*
- *concept checking*
- *collocation*
- *recycling*

REFLECTION

You are teaching an intermediate class that shares the same L1 and are at around B1 level of English. The learners tell you that they would like to learn more vocabulary. They mention topics such as money, going out for dinner, and environmental issues.

Work in groups. Choose one of the topics the learners requested and plan:

- five or six items you would teach
- what information the learners will need about each item
- how you could convey the meaning of the words
- how you could make both the spoken and written forms clear
- how you could check that the words have been understood
- how you could provide practice of the new items

Reference

Wilkins, D. (1972). *Linguistics in Language Teaching*. London: Edward Arnold.

8 The sounds of English

A Warm-up

1 Your trainer is going to give you a 'new name'. Memorize your name, but keep it secret. Your trainer will call the class register. When you hear your name, say 'Present'.

2 Think about these questions:
   a What problems might learners of English have with this activity? Why?
   b What aspect of language does the activity target?

B Sounds v letters

1 Write down the words your trainer dictates. Then check your spelling with a partner.

2 Work in pairs. Discuss the meanings of these words and see if you agree on them.

3 Count the *letters* in each word. For example:

letter = six letters (L-E-T-T-E-R)

Count the *sounds* in each word. For example:

letter = four sounds (l - e - tt - er)

4 Work in pairs. Discuss what activity B3 demonstrates about the sound-spelling relationship in English.

C Consonant sounds

1 Consonant sounds are formed when the airflow from the lungs is obstructed by the moveable parts of the mouth, including the tongue and lips. Try pronouncing these sounds, and decide where the obstruction is occurring.

You can refer to this diagram:

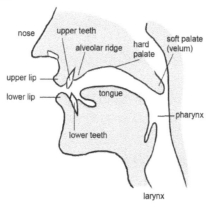

For example, the sound /b/ (as in *ban*) is articulated by obstructing the airflow at the lips.

/m/   as in *man*
/v/   as in *van*
/n/   as in *nan*
/t/   as in *tan*
/r/   as in *ran*
/k/   as in *can*

Because of the frequent mismatch between spelling and sound, it helps to use a special script (called *phonemic script*) to transcribe spoken language. Here are the 24 standard English consonant sounds in phonemic script:

CONSONANTS

	p	t	c	f	θ	s	ʃ	ʧ
voiceless	pen	town	cat	fish	think	say	she	cheese
	/pen/	/taʊn/	/kæt/	/fɪʃ/	/θɪŋk/	/seɪ/	/ʃiː/	/ʧiːz/
	b	d	g	v	ð	z	ʒ	ʤ
voiced	book	day	give	very	the	zoo	vision	jump
	/bʊk/	/deɪ/	/gɪv/	/'ver.ɪ/	/ðə/	/zuː/	/vɪʒn/	/ʤʌmp/

l	r	j	w	m	n	ŋ	h
look	run	yes	we	moon	name	sing	hand
/lʊk/	/rʌn/	/jes/	/wiː/	/muːn/	/neɪm/	/sɪŋ/	/hænd/

Cambridge International Dictionary of English

Many of the consonants consist of *voiceless* and *voiced* pairs, such as /p/ and /b/. A *voiced* sound is one that is made by activating the *vocal cords*. (You can feel them vibrate if you put your hand on your throat). To produce a *voiceless* sound, no vocal cord activation is required.

2   Read these words, using the table above.

a   /met/
b   /dek/
c   /ðen/
d   /heʤ/
e   /breθ/
f   /feʧ/
g   /nekst/
h   /jet/
i   /ʃred/
j   /ʃrɪŋk/

3 Write these words in phonemic script.

a *sent*
b *edge*
c *thin*
d *thing*
e *think*
f *this*
g *fixed*
h *jest*
i *yelled*
j *stretched*

D Vowel sounds

Vowels are formed, not by obstructing the airflow, but by modifying its passage through the mouth, principally through the use of the tongue and lips.

1 Say the vowel sounds in these words and notice any changes in the position of your tongue and lips:

Jean   June
Gin   John
Jen   Shawn
Jan

Vowels are divided between *monophthongs* (single vowels) and *diphthongs* (a glide from one vowel to another). All vowels are voiced, that is, they involve activating the vocal cords.

On the left are listed the vowels of standard British English in phonemic script. On the right are listed the vowels of standard North American English (also known as General American). In each list, monophthongs are on the left; diphthongs on the right.

British English			
iː	we	ɪə	dear
ɪ	fit	eɪ	say
ʊ	look	ʊə	sure
uː	hoot	ɔɪ	toy
e	fed	əʊ	so
ə	alone/fath<u>er</u>	eə	fair
ɜː	hurt	aɪ	die
ɔː	ought	aʊ	how
æ	hat		
ʌ	but		
ɑː	spa, tar		
ɒ	pot		

North American English			
iː	we	eɪ	say
ɪ	fit	ɔɪ	toy
ʊ	foot	oʊ	so
uː	hoot	aɪ	die
e	fed	aʊ	how
ə/ɚ	alone/fath<u>er</u>		
ɜˑ	hurt		
ɔː	oŭght		
æ	hat		
ʌ	but		
ɑː	Pa, pot		

Note that one of the commonest vowels in English is the central, unstressed vowel /ə/ – known as *schwa*.

2   Decipher these film titles, using the consonant chart and the vowel chart. Choose one variety of English.

British English	North American
a /bætmæn/	a /bætmæn/
b /kɪŋ kɒŋ/	b /kɪŋ kɑːŋ/
c /eəpleɪn/	c /erpleɪn/
d /dʒɔːz/	d /dʒɔːz/
e /ðə bɜːdz/	e /ðə bɝːdz/
f /saɪkəʊ/	f /saɪkoʊ/
g /pʌlp fɪkʃən/	g /pʌlp fɪkʃən/
h /vɜːtɪɡəʊ/	h /vɝːtɪɡoʊ/
i /ðə ʃaɪnɪŋ/	i /ðə ʃaɪnɪŋ/
j /dʒɔːz tuː/	j /dʒɔːz tuː/

3   Write these film titles in phonemic script:
   a   *Shrek*
   b   *Ben Hur*
   c   *Snatch*
   d   *Star Wars*
   e   *High Noon*
   f   *Blade Runner*
   g   *Memento*
   h   *Mystic River*

4   Work in pairs. Write two more film titles in phonemic script for your partner to decipher.

E   Contrasting languages

1   Compare these charts of the consonant sounds in English and in Thai.

English

		Place of articulation							
		Front of mouth ←--→ throat							
MANNER OF ARTICULATION	stop	p b			t d			k ɡ	
	stop + vibration					tʃ dʒ			
	through nose	m			n			ŋ	
	vibration		f v	θ ð	s z	ʃ ʒ			h
	little obstruction				r		j	w	
	sideways obstruction				l				

Thai

MANNER OF ARTICULATION		Place of articulation Front of mouth ←--→ throat							
	stop	p pʰ b			t tʰ d			k kʰ	ʔ
	stop + vibration					tɕ tɕʰ			
	through nose	m			n			ŋ	
	vibration		f		s				h
	trill				r				
	little obstruction						j	w	
	sideways obstruction				l				

Adapted from M.R. Kalaya Tingsabadh and A.S. Abramson, 1999

Which of these English word pairs might a speaker of Thai have difficulty with? Why?

a pat v bat
b fan v van
c right v light
d mess v mesh
e moss v moth
f sin v sing
g latter v ladder
h back v bag
i sigh v thigh

2 Here is an extract from a pronunciation course. Which of the above consonant distinctions does it target?

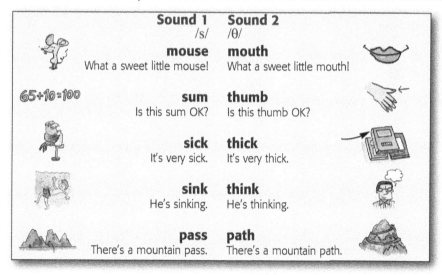

Sound 1 /s/	Sound 2 /θ/
mouse What a sweet little mouse!	**mouth** What a sweet little mouth!
sum Is this sum OK?	**thumb** Is this thumb OK?
sick It's very sick.	**thick** It's very thick.
sink He's sinking.	**think** He's thinking.
pass There's a mountain pass.	**path** There's a mountain path.

Ship or Sheep?

3 How could you use it in class? For example:

   a How would you model the two sounds?

   b How would you test students' ability to hear the difference?

   c How would you provide practice at producing the difference?

F Review

Can you answer these questions?

a How many letters are there in English?

b How many sounds are there?

c How many sounds are there in *thought*? In *six*? In *coaching*?

d How many ways is the letter 'a' pronounced in English? Clue: The tall cat ate the banana!

e What's the difference between a consonant sound and a vowel sound?

f What's the difference between the sound /s/ and the sound /z/?

g What's the name of the first and third vowel sounds in *banana*?

h What's the difference between the sound /ɪ/ in *pin*, and the sound /aɪ/ in *pine*?

i What sound do these three words have in common? *does, zoo, noise*

j What sound do these three words have in common? *first, surf, earns*

k True or false? /ʃeɪkspɪə rəʊt məkbeθ/

l True or false? /njuː jɔːk ɪz ɪn teksəs/

KEY WORDS FOR TEACHERS

Check you know the meanings of these terms.

* *phoneme, vowel, consonant, monophthong, diphthong*
* *voiced sound, unvoiced sound*
* *schwa*
* *phonemic script*
* *minimal pair*
* *RP (Received Pronunciation)*
* *GA (General American)*

REFLECTION

1 To what extent does your own variety of spoken English match the descriptions of RP or General American (GA) outlined in this unit? Are there any significant differences? Do these differences mean that some words that are different in RP or GA are pronounced the same in your variety? For example, in many varieties of New Zealand English, the words *ear* and *air* are pronounced the same. And in some varieties of North American English, such as those spoken in Canada or in and around Boston, the words *cot* and *caught* are pronounced the same, which is not generally the case in many other regions.

2 How might the variety of English that you speak affect your teaching?

References

Cambridge International Dictionary of English (1995). Cambridge: Cambridge University Press, p.1774.

Tingsabadh, M.R. Kalaya and Abramson, A. S. (1999). Thai. In *Handbook of the International Phonetic Association*, edited by the International Phonetic Association. Cambridge: Cambridge University Press, p.147.

9 Stress, rhythm and intonation

A Warm-up

1 Work in pairs. Do the activity and discuss what it demonstrates.

Imagine you are in a bar or café, and you've both just finished a drink, or a slice of chocolate cake. Have a conversation in which you both use only the word *Well*. The conversation should convey these meanings:

A: That was nice!
B: Shall we have another one?
A: I shouldn't really.
B: I'm going to have another one, even if you're not.
A: If you're going to insist …
B: You're easily persuaded – you surprise me!

2 Discuss whether learners would find this activity easy or difficult. Give reasons for your opinion.

B Stress

Stress is the prominence that is given to particular syllables (in a word) or to particular words (in an utterance).

1 Work in pairs. Read these invented words and try to predict which syllable is stressed in each one. Decide what the results of this exercise suggest about the way words are stressed in English.

pawler
veddle
malmish
pandiful
loomitive
loomition
imbelist
imbelistic
geon
geonetics
geonetology
geonetological

2 Identify six to eight vocabulary items relating to a particular theme (such as jobs, food and drink, clothing, etc) in the coursebook you are currently using with your teaching practice class. Then answer the questions.

a Which is the stressed syllable in each of these words?
b What techniques could you use to highlight the stress?

3   a   Work In pairs. Mark the main stressed syllable in the second part (i.e. after the |) of each of the
        following sayings and catchphrases. Then answer the question.

    i   Don't worry | be happy.
    ii   You win some | and you lose some.
    iii   You can run | but you can't hide.
    iv   It's not what you know | it's who you know.
    v   Don't just stand there | do something.
    vi   The bigger they are | the harder they fall.
    vii Two steps forward | one step back.
    viii You scratch my back | and I'll scratch yours.

   b   What determines which word is stressed?

4   Study this coursebook activity. How does your answer to the last exercise apply to this one? (Note that
    'the words in pink' are: *Susie owns a flat in Leeds.*)

HELP WITH PRONUNCIATION
Stress and rhythm (4): emphasis and meaning

 a   CD3 ▶ 24 Listen to these sentences. Notice how
the extra stress on one word affects the meaning.

  1   I **THOUGHT** Ann would come.
     (She's here. My prediction was right.)
  2   I thought Ann would **COME**.
     (She's not here. My prediction was wrong.)

  b   Listen again and practise.

 a   Read the sentence in pink. Then match
responses 1–5 to meanings a–e.

Susie owns a flat in Leeds.

  1   I think she's **RENTING** it.
  2   I **THOUGHT** she owned that flat.
  3   **JAMES** owns that flat.
  4   I thought she owned a **HOUSE** there.
  5   I think the flat's in **BRADFORD**.

  a   Tom said she didn't, but I knew I was right.
  b   I don't think she owns it.
  c   You're thinking of the wrong person.
  d   I don't think it's in Leeds.
  e   I don't think it's a flat.

  b   CD3 ▶ 25 Listen and check.

  c   Listen again. Take turns to say the sentence
in pink in **2a** and responses 1–5 and a–e.

---

face2face Upper Intermediate

C Rhythm

1 Work in pairs. Take turns to read aloud the following sentences so that each sentence takes the same number of beats as the first sentence (which you should read fairly slowly and deliberately). Repeat each sentence before moving to the next. It may help to beat the rhythm with your hand. Then answer the questions.

■	■	■
Words	take	stress.
Words	should take	stress.
Words	should take	the stress.
Some words	should take	the stress.
Some words	should've taken	the stress.
Some of the words	should've taken	the stress.

1 What happens to the individual words as the sentence becomes longer?
2 Why might this create a problem for students – in terms of both listening and speaking?

2 Work in pairs. Study this coursebook activity.

1 Decide what aspect of pronunciation it targets.
2 Discuss how this aspect of pronunciation might be connected with rhythm.

HELP WITH PRONUNCIATION

1 **CD2** 44 Work in pairs. How do we say these strong and weak forms? Listen and check. Listen again and practise.

strong	weak	strong	weak
was /wɒz/	was /wəz/	does /dʌz/	does /dəz/
were /wɜː/	were /wə/	do /duː/	do /də/

2 **a** Work in pairs. Look at this conversation. Do we usually say the strong (S) or weak (W) forms of the words in blue?

A Sorry we're late. We [1]were (W) having lunch. Right, [2]do ( ) we need anything for the meeting?

B Yes, we [3]do ( ). We need these reports. [4]Does ( ) Lisa know about the meeting?

A Yes, she [5]does ( ).

B OK. [6]Were ( ) you at the last meeting?

A Yes, we [7]were ( ).

B [8]Was ( ) it a very long meeting?

A Yes, it [9]was ( ).

B What [10]was ( ) it about?

A I don't know. I [11]was ( ) asleep!

b **CD2** 45 Listen and check. When do we use the strong and weak forms of the words in **1**?

c Work in pairs. Practise the conversation.

face2face Pre-intermediate

D Intonation

> Most learners of English as an additional language [...] are not taught intonation and do not study intonation. Yet they do not speak English on a monotone. [...] How can this be?
>
> It must be because the principles of intonation in language are sufficiently universal for us to be able to rely on them even in a foreign language.
>
> J.C. Wells, 2014

1 Work in pairs. Say each of these sentences aloud in two different ways, conveying two different meanings.

  1 What is the difference in meaning, in each case?
  2 How is this difference conveyed?

For example: *I like Chinese art and opera*

  1 I like | Chinese art and opera| (= Chinese art and Chinese opera)
  2 I like | Chinese art| and opera| (= Chinese art and any kind of opera)

    a the people who left suddenly started running
    b when shall we eat grandma
    c the mouse which ate the cheese escaped
    d he's a nurse
    e Sigrid is not Swedish is she
    f I'll have it with ham basil olives pineapple
    g hi
    h thanks a million

2 In the light of the above exercise, identify ways that intonation affects meaning.

3 Study this coursebook material and answer the questions.

a ▶1.38 Listen to the examples. Does the tone go up (↗) or down (↘) on the question tag? What's the difference in meaning?

  1 No, it isn't very quick, is it?
  2 No, they weren't helpful, were they?
  3 Yes, you need to make things easy, don't you?

b Practise saying the exchanges in 2e. Try to use the correct tone in the reply.

c Discuss people and things you and other students know – for example, a person, a café, a film or a car. Use the adjectives below and question tags to agree.

- amusing – funny
- cheerful – happy
- interesting – fascinating
- frightening – terrifying
- exhausting – tiring

That photo is really striking.

Yes, it's stunning, isn't it?

Empower B2

1 What feature of intonation does the material target?
2 Look at exercises a and c again. Which of the following activities would be useful after a and before c?
   a A 'read aloud' task, where learners read a number of sentences that include question tags, attempting to apply the appropriate intonation.
   b A gap-fill exercise where learners write in the missing question tag.
   c A dialogue activity, in which learners write dialogues that include question tags, and then perform them.

KEY WORDS FOR TEACHERS

Check you know the meanings of these terms.

- *stress (word stress, sentence stress)*
- *rhythm*
- *strong and weak forms*
- *intonation*

REFLECTION

Discuss these questions in pairs or groups.
1 Which of the following areas do you think is most critical in ensuring communicative effectiveness? Why?
   a accurate production of individual sounds (i.e. vowels and consonants)
   b accurate stress placement in words
   c accurate stress placement in utterances
   d native-like rhythm
   e accurate use of intonation
2 Which of the above areas do you think is the most easily learnable? Why?

Reference

J.C. Wells (2014) *Sounds Interesting: Observations on English and general phonetics*. Cambridge University Press, p.133.

10 Teaching pronunciation

A Warm-up

1 What impact might pronunciation have on each of these areas of learners' English?

- Speaking
- Listening
- Reading
- Writing
- Grammar
- Vocabulary

2 Work in pairs. Discuss these statements and decide to what extent you agree.

a It is important for teachers to use only standard British or American English in the classroom.
b Intelligibility (i.e. being understood) is more important than sounding like a native speaker.
c When working on pronunciation, the priority is for students to be able to say things correctly themselves.
d Problems with pronunciation are unlikely to cause communication breakdowns.

B Pronunciation exercises

1 Study the pronunciation activities (A–D) below and answer the questions.

- What aspect of pronunciation is each activity targeting? Is it a 'small' feature (such as individual sounds) or a 'big' feature (such as sentence stress or intonation)?
- Is the objective of the activity *reception* or *production* (or both)?
- Is the feature used in context or is it decontextualized?
- How communicative is the activity? Could non-communicative activities be adapted to make them more communicative?

A	The teacher demonstrates the difference in pronunciation of the *-ed* ending on *worked, lived* and *started*. She then asks learners to make three columns in their books, headed by /t/, /d/, and /ɪd/ respectively. She reads out a list of past tense words, e.g. *opened, walked, moved, lifted, missed, waited*, etc.; the students write each one in the appropriate column.
B	Learners have cards made up of pairs of rhyming words, e.g. *steak, make; do, true*, etc. In groups, learners take turns to show the cards; if a card rhymes with the preceding card, the player keeps the pair. The winner is the player with the most pairs.
C	Learners prepare cards with different types of gift, e.g. a bunch of flowers; a broken pencil; a house, etc. Learners hand each other cards, saying 'Here's a present for you.' . The receiver should respond by saying 'Thank you' in a way that is proportionate to their gratitude for the gift.
D	The teacher sets up a speaking activity, e.g. dialogue, role play, chat, etc, then rotates around the groups. When students make a mistake in their pronunciation which the teacher hears, she/he says, or indicates, 'I'm sorry, I don't understand.'. The student attempts to repair the error.

2 Work in groups. Evaluate the activities in B1. For example, discuss whether you would like to do them as a learner. Decide how they might help learners with one of the areas you discussed in A1. Give reasons.

C Techniques for teaching pronunciation

1 The table shows a variety of techniques which a teacher can use in any lesson to draw learners' attention to pronunciation or to provide pronunciation practice.

Work with a partner. Read the technique. Suggest an aim or stages in a lesson when a teacher might use each of these techniques. There may be multiple answers.

Technique	Aim	When a teacher might use it
Showing learners the shape of your mouth and position of your tongue when producing a specific phoneme (sound).	For learners to notice the physical changes in the mouth necessary to produce specific sounds.	
Displaying a word in both the written form and phonemic script, e.g. *comb* /kəʊm/		When introducing a new vocabulary item with an unusual sound-spelling relationship, for example silent letters. As part of error correction after a speaking or writing activity.
Writing out a word in normal script, putting dots between the syllables, and underlining the stressed syllable, e.g. *e·mer·gen·cy*.	To show learners how many syllables a word has and which syllable carries the stress.	
Indicating on your fingers how many words there are in a sentence, then putting your fingers together to show where there are contractions. Learners repeat the sentence with the contracted form.		After a speaking activity, as a way of helping learners to produce spoken language more fluently. When modelling a sentence to introduce a new grammar pattern, e.g. present perfect: *She's been to China*.
Substitution drill, i.e. T: *I'm going shopping. We* SS: *We're going shopping.* T: *not* SS: *We aren't going shopping.*, etc.	For learners to verbally manipulate the form of a grammar structure they have just been introduced to, including features such as contractions.	
Writing out a sentence from a listening transcript and highlighting features of connected speech on it.		Before a listening activity, to draw attention to potentially problematic features. After a listening activity, particularly if learners have misheard something in the audio – this can be used to focus on an individual answer.

2 Have you observed teachers using any of these techniques during your course so far? What other techniques or activities have you observed for working on pronunciation?

D Anticipating problems

1 Work in pairs. Discuss the pronunciation problems learners might have with these syllabus areas.

a *can/can't* (to talk about ability)
(Possible problem: failure to discriminate between weak and strong forms, so that *can* sounds like *can't* ...)
b ordinal numbers, i.e. *first, second, third, fourth,* etc.
c *used to* (to talk about past habits)
d present simple questions, e.g. *Where does she live? What do you do?*
e polite requests using *Would you mind ...-ing?*
f clothing vocabulary, e.g. *shirt, shorts, suit, shoes, jacket, overcoat, scarf, pullover,* etc.

2 Your trainer will assign you one of the above areas. Think of classroom solutions to the problems that learners might have. Consider both recognition and production of the language. For example:

a *can/can't*
Possible solution: the teacher repeats one of the words several times and then changes to the other word. Learners have to stop the teacher when they hear the change – *can can can can can't can't can't can't can,* etc. (learners could then do this in pairs).

E Planning pronunciation work

Here is a section from a coursebook. The learners have completed some comprehension work based on a photostory, then moved on to these activities to focus on the language. No explicit pronunciation work has been included. Decide where you think it would be appropriate to include some work on pronunciation in this lesson and what form this could take.

WordWise
Expressions with *good*

1 **Use the phrases in the list to complete these sentences from the unit so far.**

~~for good~~ | So far, so good | not very good at
It's no good | It's a good thing | it's all good

0 The lights have stopped animals coming to the farm *for good* .

1 I'm _____ creative thinking.

2 That's five words. _____ .

3 She gave me an A minus, best I've ever got! So _____ .

4 _____ . I just can't get the keys out.

5 _____ Emma's such a nice person.

2 **Which phrase means:**

1 for ever

2 It's not successful.

3 Everything is all right.

4 We have started but not finished, but everything has been OK until now.

5 not talented at

6 I'm/We're/You're lucky that …

Workbook page 38

FUNCTIONS
Expressing frustration

1 **Read the photostory again. Which of these things does Emma not say? What do all the sentences have in common?**

1 I can't (do that).
2 I'm hopeless (at …)
3 This is hopeless!
4 No chance.

5 I give up.
6 I'll never (come up with anything).
7 This is pointless.

2 **Think about the woman who loses her keys. Write three things she might have thought using the expressions in Exercise 1.**

I'll never get the keys out.

Think 4

KEY WORDS FOR TEACHERS

Check you know the meanings of these terms.

- *phonemic script*
- *intelligibility*
- *connected speech*
- *receptive skills*
- *productive skills*
- *accent*
- *standard (British/American/etc.) English*
- *English as a Lingua Franca (ELF), English as an International Language (EIL)*

REFLECTION

1 List three reasons why it could be important or useful for you to include pronunciation work in lessons.
2 List three problems learners in your current TP group might have with pronunciation. Say what you could do to help your learners improve.

Compare your ideas with a partner.

11 Phrases and sentences

A Warm-up

Game: work in teams. How many well-formed sentences can you make out of these words? You don't have to use all the words in each sentence, but you can't use any word twice in the same sentence.

after cat very dog chased by was the a frightened when running it probably

You have three minutes. You get one point for the first word of each sentence, two for the second, three for the third, and so on.

Discuss: What kind of knowledge did you need to be able to play this game?

B Phrases

Words group together to form meaningful units called *phrases*. Phrases cluster around a head word, which may be one of five different parts of speech: noun, verb, adjective, adverb or preposition.

1 Work in pairs. Each of these film titles forms a phrase. Identify the head word: this should tell you what kind of phrase it is.

1 *On the Waterfront = head word 'on': prepositional phrase*
2 *The Silence of the Lambs*
3 *Get Out*
4 *Cheaper by the Dozen*
5 *Nowhere to Hide*
6 *Crazy Rich Asians*
7 *In the Heat of the Night*
8 *Counter Clockwise*
9 *Absolutely Fabulous*
10 *Don't Look Back*
11 *Too Hot to Handle*
12 *The Spy who Came in from the Cold*
13 *Before Midnight*

2 Look at the sentences you generated in the warm-up game. Can you find examples of different types of phrases?

C The noun phrase

Noun phrases (NPs) in English have at least four elements, only one of which – the head – is obligatory. The other elements are: determiners (such as articles, numbers), premodification (such as adjectives), and postmodification, i.e. all the items after the head.

For example:

Determiner	Premodification	Head	Postmodification
The		Silence	of the Lambs
	Crazy Rich	Asians	
The		Spy	who Came in from the Cold

1 Work in pairs. Can you complete the table, using these film titles?

1 *The Spy Who Loved Me*
2 *Murder on the Orient Express*
3 *My Beautiful Laundrette*
4 *Airplane*
5 *Rosemary's Baby*
6 *A Streetcar Named Desire*
7 *The Bridges of Madison County*
8 *55 Days at Peking*
9 *Star Trek*
10 *Much Ado About Nothing*

Determiner	Premodification	Head	Postmodification

2 What kinds of words or phrases go into each column? For example, articles (*the, a*) typically go into the determiner column.

3 Based on this activity, what problems do you think learners might have with noun phrases in English?

D Sentence elements

Each phrase in a sentence forms an element that fulfils a specific *function*. For example:

A funny thing	happened	on the way to the forum
SUBJECT	VERB	ADVERBIAL
(identifies the actor or agent)	(typically expresses a process or state)	(gives circumstantial information, such as time, place or manner)

I	married	a monster from outer space
SUBJECT	VERB	OBJECT
		(identifies the person or thing affected)

I	was	a teenage werewolf
SUBJECT	VERB	COMPLEMENT
		(gives additional information about the subject)

There are five sentence elements in all: SUBJECT, VERB, OBJECT, COMPLEMENT and ADVERBIAL.

Work in pairs. Divide these film titles into their component phrases and assign a function to each phrase slot. (Note that sometimes a phrase slot can contain only one word).

1 *It Happened One Night*
2 *Mr. Smith Goes to Washington*
3 *Gentlemen Prefer Blondes*
4 *The Empire Strikes Back*
5 *That's Entertainment*
6 *The Russians are Coming*
7 *Meet Me in St Louis*
8 *Who Framed Roger Rabbit?*
9 *Batman Returns*

E Contrastive analysis

1 Read the sentences with their translations and answer the questions.

1 Are the elements in the sentence (e.g. subject, verb, object) in the same order or a different one?

2 Are the elements in a phrase (e.g. article, adjective, noun) in the same order or a different one?

3 Are there elements that occur in English but not in the other language – and vice versa?

A. **Turkish**

ingilizce	kitapları	odamda
English	books-the	room-my-in

(The English books are in my room)

Biz	yine	eski	hayatımıza	döndük
We	again	old	life-our-to	returned

(We returned to our old life again)

B. **Arabic**

buyūtu	ar rajuli	al-ghanīyi	ɛalā	nahrin
houses	the man	the rich	on	river

(The rich man's houses are on a river)

hādhā	khitābun	ba'athathu	sayyidatun	shahīratun
this	letter	sent-it	lady	famous

(This is a letter which a famous lady sent)

C. **Japanese**

ringo-o	tabeta
apple-[OBJECT marker]	ate

(I ate an apple)

zō-wa	hana-ga	nagai
elephant-[TOPIC marker]	nose-[SUBJECT marker]	long

(Elephants have long noses)

watashi-wa	mise-e	ikimasu
I-[TOPIC marker]	store-to	go

(I go to the store)

Hanako-ga	Taro-ni kompyūtā-o	ageta
Hanako-[SUBJECT marker]	Taro-to computer-[OBJECT marker]	gave

(Hanako gave Taro a computer)

2 Work in pairs. Discuss what errors speakers of each language in activity E3 might make in English.

KEY WORDS FOR TEACHERS

Check you know the meanings of these terms.

- *(adjective/adverb/prepositional) phrase*
- *noun phrase, head word, pre-/post modification, relative clause*
- *subject, verb, object, adverbial, complement*

REFLECTION

Think of a language other than English that you are familiar with. (If you don't speak another language, you can search for information online about a language you might be interested in learning, or whose speakers you might be teaching in the future.) In what ways is this language similar to / different from English, with regard to its syntax, e.g. parts of speech and word order? What difficulties might this present to a speaker of that language who is learning English?

12 Tense and aspect

A Warm-up

Here is an activity from an intermediate-level coursebook. Do it individually and then compare in pairs.

C   **Choose five time expressions from the box and write sentences that are true for you.**

at the moment	at 8 o'clock this morning	never	every day
last year	for the last three months	now	once a week
since I was a child	when I got home	yesterday	

Evolve 4

1   How many of your sentences are the same or similar?

2   Can you identify any of the verb forms you each used? For example: '*At the moment I'm training to be a teacher.' I am training = present continuous*

B Tense review

1   Here is a table of English verb forms. Can you complete it?

	simple	continuous (aspect)	perfect (aspect)	perfect continuous (aspects)
present (tense)	*they work*		*they have worked*	
past (tense)		*they were working*		*they had been working*

2   Here is a text from an intermediate level coursebook.

FIVE THINGS ABOUT ME

Here is my answer to the latest blog challenge!
(If I **get 1,000 likes**, my boss will donate $1,000 to charity. So please like my list!)

1 Every year I **set myself a goal** of learning a new skill. I've done a lot of different things. Last year I learned to play chess. This year I've been learning computer animation and design.

2 People tell me I **have a great sense of humor**, and I love to **tell jokes**!

3 A few years ago, while I was working at a summer camp, a girl came screaming out of her cabin because she saw a huge spider on her bed. I hate spiders, but I **faced my fear**, went in there, and caught that spider. I felt so brave! 😏

4 I'm saving money to open a small studio where I can teach art classes. I've always wanted to **run my own business**. I love **working with my hands**, and I want to do something I can really **take pride in**.

5 This year I'm going to **run a marathon**. I don't want to **win a medal** or **break a record** or anything. I just want to finish! I'm sure I can **rise to the challenge**!

Evolve 4

Find examples in the text of at least six of the structures listed in B1. For example:

	simple	continuous (aspect)	perfect (aspect)	perfect continuous (aspects)
present (tense)	*get, set, have*		*have done*	
past (tense)	*learned, came*			

3 Here is a coursebook task that relates to the text in the preceding activity. Work in pairs to complete it.

---

3 **GRAMMAR: Tense review (simple and continuous)**

A **Complete the descriptions of different tenses. Use the sentences in the grammar box to help you.**
Which tense describes …

1 past experiences with no specific past time given?   *present perfect*
2 an action in progress in the past?
3 a completed action in the past?
4 a habit or repeated action in the present?
5 an action in progress in the present?
6 an action that started sometime in the past and is still continuing?

Simple and continuous tenses	
simple present	Every year I **set** myself a goal of learning a new skill.
present continuous	I'm **saving** money to open a small studio.
simple past	I **faced** my fear, **went** in there, and **caught** that spider.
past continuous	I **was working** in a summer camp when it happened.
present perfect	I've **done** a lot of different things.
present perfect continuous	This year I've **been learning** computer animation.

Evolve 4

C Tense v aspect

Coursebooks (like the one in the previous task) use the term 'tense' broadly to describe the combinations above. Technically, though, verb forms like present continuous and past perfect are not different tenses, but different combinations of tense plus aspect. So: present continuous = present tense + continuous aspect; past perfect = past tense + perfect aspect.

Look at these paired examples (taken from a corpus of naturally-occurring language). In each case, name the underlined verb forms and decide what the aspect – either continuous or perfect – adds to the meaning.

a Swasey, who has two young children, <u>works </u>from home two days a week.
b DH <u>is working</u> from home today and helped get the kids ready.

c Early the next morning I <u>drove</u> to the cemetery.
d On Sept. 25, he <u>was driving</u> to work when ATF agents stopped him.

e 'Music is my life, and I <u>love</u> it.'
f I'm reading *Gotham Diaries* now, and I'<u>m loving</u> it!

g As a child, he <u>learned</u> to knit sweaters for himself.
h So far in his life, he <u>has learned</u> Bahasa Indonesia, Sudanese, Irish Gaelic, Mandarin Chinese …

i Bergman <u>made</u> films about the apocalyptic nature of war.
j The 55-year-old Vendetti <u>has made</u> films and videos for 15 years.

k Someone <u>wrote</u> 'Californians Go Home' in the dust on their moving truck.
l On the facade, someone <u>has written</u> 'Proud to be Black'.

D Learner problems

Here is a composition written by a Brazilian learner of English. Her teacher has underlined some of the verb phrase errors.
1 Can you correct them?
2 Can you explain your corrections?

1   I was born in Osasco, the city located near the big São Paulo. I lived in Osasco until my 10 years
2   old and I still <u>had</u> wonderful memories from this epoch. Then my father's job was transferred
3   and <u>we've moved</u> to Conchas, one very small city located about two hours from Osasco.
4   When I completed 15 years old we all moved to Itapetininga. This city is farther and bigger
5   than Conchas, so it <u>doesn't looks</u> like a country city. There I got my first job and I had my
6   first date too. Then in 2006, I quit my job and <u>come</u> back to Osasco. In the middle of 2006, I
7   started the course of Law and during this time <u>I've been living</u> with my grandmother. <u>She has</u>
8   <u>moved</u> to Osasco when my grandfather dead. Finally, with a lot of struggle, in 2015 I bought
9   my apartment. It's small but very warm and confortable. <u>I've lived</u> there alone. When you live
10 alone <u>you're having</u> a lot of advantages and disadvantages, but in my opinion it's really worth!

E Materials

Study these teaching materials.

a What verb form does each one target?
b What exact meaning is targeted?
c Is the focus on form or meaning – or both?

1

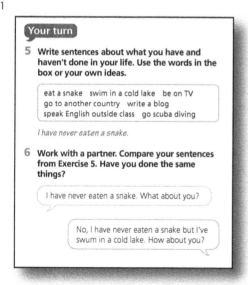

Eyes Open A2

2

English Grammar in Use

2.3 Complete the sentences using these verbs. Sometimes you need the negative.

| believe | eat | flow | go | grow | make | rise | tell | translate |

1 The earth ....*goes*.... round the sun.
2 Rice ....*doesn't grow*.... in cold climates.
3 The sun .... in the east.
4 Bees .... honey.
5 Vegetarians .... meat.
6 An atheist .... in God.

7 An interpreter .... from one language into another.
8 Liars are people who .... the truth.
9 The River Amazon .... into the Atlantic Ocean.

3

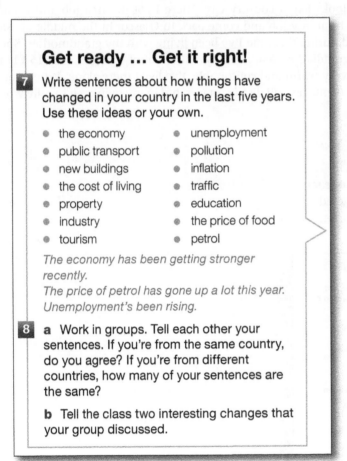

Get ready ... Get it right!

7 Write sentences about how things have changed in your country in the last five years. Use these ideas or your own.

- the economy
- public transport
- new buildings
- the cost of living
- property
- industry
- tourism

- unemployment
- pollution
- inflation
- traffic
- education
- the price of food
- petrol

The economy has been getting stronger recently.
The price of petrol has gone up a lot this year.
Unemployment's been rising.

8 **a** Work in groups. Tell each other your sentences. If you're from the same country, do you agree? If you're from different countries, how many of your sentences are the same?

b Tell the class two interesting changes that your group discussed.

face2face Upper Intermediate

F Classroom application

Work in groups. Your trainer will assign your group one of the grammar items (a–f). Devise a way of presenting this item.

a present simple with adverbs of frequency (such as *always, often, sometimes, never*)
b present continuous for activities in progress at the time of speaking
c present continuous for future arrangements
d present perfect for recent events, using *just*
e present perfect for situations continuing to the present, using *for/since* …
f present perfect for changes that have present results (for example: *They've painted the town hall*)

Your presentation should include:

• a situation which illustrates the meaning of the item
• at least three or four examples of the item
• some kind of check of understanding, such as concept questions or timelines

Identify any visual aids that would facilitate your presentation.

Be prepared to demonstrate your presentation idea to the rest of the class.

KEY WORDS FOR TEACHERS

Check you know the meanings of these terms.

• *tense, aspect*
• *continuous (aspect), perfect (aspect)*
• *auxiliary verb*
• *present simple, present continuous, present perfect*
• *past simple, past continuous, past perfect*
• *stative verbs, dynamic verbs*
• *corpus*

REFLECTION

Revisit the sentences you wrote for the warm-up activity.
a Can you now identify all the verb forms that you used?
b What tense + aspect combinations are commonly associated with the different time expressions in the exercise?
Note: Consult the *Brief Guide to the English Verb* in the appendix on page 212.

13 Language functions

A Warm-up

1   Here are some well-known quotations or catchphrases. Can you match them to their function – i.e. their communicative purpose?

1	Round up the usual suspects.	a	warning
2	I'll have what she's having.	b	inviting
3	My name is Bond, James Bond.	c	commanding
4	Houston, we have a problem.	d	introducing
5	It'll be all right on the night.	e	checking
6	Doctor Livingstone, I presume?	f	requesting
7	Come up and see me sometime.	g	reassuring

2   Identify any grammar structures that you are already familiar with in any of the quotes. For example, in (4) the present form of the verb *have* is used. Is there an obvious connection between the grammar and the function?

3   Each quote represents what was said in a specific location by one specific person to one or more others. How good is your general knowledge? In each case:

   a what was the context of the utterance? i.e. where were the speakers and what were they talking about?
   b what was the relationship between the speaker and the person(s) addressed?

   If you do not know the sources of these quotes, can you suggest a context in which they might have been said. Who would say it to whom, for example?

> For learners, probably the most striking way in which the knowledge of language developed through a grammatical syllabus fails to measure up to their communicational needs is in its lack of situational relevance. They may […] have considerable practical command of grammatical structures, but the language that they rehearse in the classroom will be inadequately related to what is needed in the situations in which they may actually want to use the language.
>
> David Wilkins, 1976

B Context and function

1   How many different ways could this sign be expressed in words? Work in pairs.

2   What factors would determine the choice of the different expressions in B1? What might determine the order you would teach them in?

3   Look at the situations below where the same sentence is spoken in four different contexts. Decide on the function of the sentence in each case.

    It's ten past nine.

4 Think of at least two different possible contexts and two corresponding functions for each of the following utterances:

   a I'll call the police.
   b It's cold in here.
   c That's your phone.
   d Can you drive?

Function, style and language

1 The choice between one of several different ways of performing a language function depends on a number of context factors. These factors will include such things as whether the message is spoken or written. Another key factor is the relationship between the people involved, such as how well they know each other, or the social distance between them. The effect of these different adjustments to context factors is known as *register*, which can be formal or informal, for example. Decide on suitable utterances for the context described in the table:

Function	Context and utterance
1 *inviting*	a Send a text message inviting your new neighbours for a welcome drink at your apartment.
	b You want to have a drink with your friend after work. You say: '...'
2 *asking a favour*	c You want to borrow your flatmate's phone charger. You say: '...'
	d You are expecting a package to be delivered the next day but you won't be at home. You phone a neighbour whom you don't know very well and leave a voicemail message, asking them if they could take delivery of it. You say: '...'
3 *making a suggestion*	e Your local gym has no wi-fi connection. Write a short note on the subject for the gym's 'suggestion box'.
	f A work colleague is suffering from back pain, which you think is caused by the way their computer monitor is positioned. You say: '...'

There are particular ways of expressing many functions that have become conventionalized. For example, *Would you like [an X]?* typically functions as an offer. These *formulaic expressions* are often included in syllabuses, alongside grammar items.

2 Put the formulaic expressions in their correct place in this extract from an elementary syllabus.

Functions	Formulaic expressions
1 asking permission	
2 polite requests	
3 apologizing, and making excuses	
4 asking and giving opinions	

a *What was X like?*   c *I had to …*   e *I thought it was really …*
b *Could you … , please?*   d *Can I … , please?*   f *I'm sorry I didn't …*

3 Work in pairs. Study the coursebook you are using with your teaching practice class. Find the syllabus for the course, which is usually located at the front of the book. Does it include ways of expressing different functions?

D Materials for teaching functional language

Here is an extract from a coursebook, focusing on the language of suggestions.

1 What use could you make of the picture?
2 How would you stage part B?
3 Why is some of the conversation in bold?
4 How would you focus on these items in class?
5 How could you provide practice using these items?

---

1 FUNCTIONAL LANGUAGE

A **Jonathan is in Mexico City for a meeting with his coworker, Antonio. They're making plans to go out in the evening. What do you think they are saying?**

B 🔊 **2.34** **Read and listen. Where are Antonio and Jonathan going to have dinner? Where are they going to meet? What time are they going to meet?**

🔊 2.34 Audio script

Antonio	So, Jonathan, **why don't we go out tonight?**
Jonathan	**OK, sounds good.**
Antonio	Do you like Mexican food?
Jonathan	I love it! Are there any good Mexican restaurants in town?
Antonio	Um, in Mexico City? Yeah, I know one or two places!
Jonathan	I'm sure you do!
Antonio	There's a very good restaurant near your hotel. **Why don't we go there?**
Jonathan	**Good idea.**
Antonio	So **let's meet at the hotel.**
Jonathan	OK. What time? Eight o'clock?
Antonio	Um … **I'm sorry, but I can't.** How about eight-thirty?
Jonathan	**Yes, sure.**

Evolve 1

Your trainer will show you how the material is developed in the coursebook. Did you have the same or similar ideas?

E Teaching functions

1   Work in groups. Your trainer will assign each group a language function (such as *apologizing*) and a level (such as *beginners*). With your group, create a short lesson as follows:

- Think of *two* situations in which the function might typically occur, one more formal than the other.
- Choose an appropriate way of expressing this function for each of the two situations.
- Write two short dialogues (6–8 lines) which contextualize the functional expressions you have chosen.
- Work out how you would use these dialogues to present and contrast the functional expressions to a class at the relevant level.

Be prepared to demonstrate your lesson to the rest of the class.

KEY WORDS FOR TEACHERS

Check you know the meanings of these terms.

- *(communicative) function*
- *context, register*
- *appropriacy*
- *formulaic expression*

REFLECTION

A *functional approach* to language teaching emerged as a reaction to a purely *formal approach* – that is, the teaching of grammar forms or structures, irrespective of the way they are used.

a   What sort of problems might a learner encounter who had been taught only language forms, and not their associated functions?

b   On the other hand, what might the drawbacks be of organizing a course solely around language functions?

c   Can you think of specific instances in your own experience, either as a second language user or as a teacher, where communication was impaired because of *inappropriate* (rather than *inaccurate*) language use?

Reference

Wilkins, D. (1976). *Notional Syllabuses*. Oxford: Oxford University Press, p.12.

14 Text and discourse

A Warm-up

1 Your trainer will give you the first line of a text. Listen to the instructions and do the activity.

2 Read the text that you started and answer the questions.

1 Do you like the text?
2 Does it make sense?
3 Does it hold together, i.e. is it cohesive?

3 Compare ideas with a partner.

B Connected text

1 Work in groups of three. Look at the first line of a story, then read the sentences a–e, and put them in the right order to complete the text.

Once upon a time there was a farmer who dug up a big earthenware jar in his field.
a So the man sold the brushes, and the family managed to live quite comfortably.
b No matter how many were taken out, others kept on taking their place.
c But while the boy was brushing the inside of the jar, he dropped the brush inside and the jar suddenly began to fill with brushes.
d So he carried it home and asked his son to clean it out.
e 'This will make a fine jar for storing rice,' he said to himself.

2 Your trainer will show you a copy of the text. Check that your version matches the original. If not, account for any differences.

3 Work in pairs. Discuss what kinds of knowledge you drew on to be able to order the sentences.

C Cohesion

1 Work in pairs. Look at the sentences in B2 again and identify the ways that each sentence connected to the one before it.

2 Read this summary of the main lexical and grammatical ways a text can be made cohesive. Then read the rest of the folk tale and find at least one example of these cohesive devices. Compare with a partner.

Lexical:
* repetition of words, or words from the same word family (e.g. *brushing – brush – brushes*)
* use of general words to refer to something more specific that is mentioned elsewhere (e.g. *a farmer – the man; his son – the boy*)
* use of words from the same lexical set (*farmer – field – rice*)
* leaving a word out because it can be recovered from the previous text, as in *No matter how many [brushes] were taken out …* (this is called 'ellipsis')
* substitution of previously mentioned words with pronouns: *… others kept on taking their place.*

Grammatical:

- reference using pronouns: *So he carried it home and asked his son to clean it out.*
- back reference using different determiners, such as the definite article (*the jar*) or possessives (*his son*)
- linkers, such as *So ... But ...*

Some time later, while they were shovelling out brushes, a coin fell into the jar by mistake. At once the brushes disappeared and the jar began to fill with money. So now the family became rich, for they could take as much money out of the jar as ever they wished.

Now, the man had an old grandfather at home, who was weak and shaky. Since they needed as many hands as possible, his grandson set the poor man to work shovelling money out of the jar. One day, however, the old man's strength gave out, and he toppled into the jar and died. At once the money disappeared, and the whole jar began to fill itself with dead grandfathers. The farmer had to pull them out one by one and have them buried. For this purpose he had to spend all the money he had gained. So, in a rage, he took a brick and smashed the jar, and he was now just as poor as he once had been.

3   Work in pairs. Look at these exercises from two coursebooks. What aspects of cohesion does each one focus on?

a

In this lesson, you ...
- plan an argument.
- contrast ideas.
- avoid errors with *whereas*.

Task   Write a script for an online debate.
Should employers judge applicants by their online profiles?

A   **Brainstorm**   Read the question above. Write three reasons to answer "yes" and three reasons to answer "no."

B   **Look at a model**   Read the debate script. Circle three more expressions that contrast ideas.

> Many employers check the Internet for information about job applicants. However, this is not a fair way to judge a person. On the one hand, employers need people who will fit into the company. An online profile gives information that employers will not see on a résumé – for example, if the person is aggressive or has extreme views. On the other hand, an online profile is for friends, whereas a résumé is for employers. A résumé provides the most relevant details about qualifications and work experience. An online profile may contain information that employers should not use to judge an applicant, such as age or religion. In conclusion, while there are good reasons to check an applicant's online profile, it is not a professional document. For this reason, it is not fair, in my opinion, to judge candidates by their personal online profiles.

Viewpoint 1

b

With a partner, use reference words from the box to replace the underlined words.

This   They   He   She   Them   It   These

1 We need to make an effort to understand how things work in other cultures. <u>The effort</u> is the first step to effective communication across cultures.
2 Many presenters like to use gestures. <u>Gestures</u> help the audience to follow the flow of a presentation.
3 Using idioms in a presentation can cause trouble. <u>Idioms</u> can sometimes have two meanings.
4 I had a conversation with a Malaysian woman. <u>The Malaysian woman</u> told me a story about a presentation that went wrong.

Business Explorer 2

D Coherence

1 Read the text below and decide what is wrong with it.

Once upon a time there were two brothers, who lived in the same house. The house known as 'Inde Steenrotse', situated on the Dwars Quay at Middelburg, dated 1590, is noteworthy for its large panels in high relief. For this relief, much thanks. Our thanks are also due to Jill Florent and Penny Hands for their editorial expertise. I recognized the faces of the two last-named, but I had not, until Morton informed me, known who they were. And since that time no one ever heard from Old Dschang again.

2 How does this text support the argument that a text may be cohesive but not coherent?

E Putting it into practice

1 Read this example of learner writing and answer the questions.

Dear Sir or Madam,

I would like to express you what is my opinion about the programmes you are showing through our local TV Channel. I supose you are not psicologist, you are 'only' a manager, but I think any person should know that TV is a mass-media you should use to release information, entertainment, culture, or anything like this. But you did not get it, and you use TV as a gun, as a weapon, trying to scare everyone who lays in his comfortable sofa, waiting for an only acceptable TV programme just to spend the last few day hours relaxed.

In the other hand we can choose between another kind of clever and interesting programmes such as a Miss World Award or the terrific Scotch Whisky manufacturing story.

Please sir, I would be very grateful if you take out this horrible productions from our little image cages we have in front of the sofa.

Your's faithfully
---

a How cohesive is it? (= Does it hang together?)
b How coherent is it? (= Does it make sense?)

2 Work in pairs. Decide how you could help the learner improve the cohesion and coherence of the text in activity E1.

KEY WORDS FOR TEACHERS

Check you know the meanings of these terms.

- *cohesion, coherence*
- *reference*
- *ellipsis, substitution*
- *linkers*
- *genre*

REFLECTION

Read the text that you started (and which your classmates continued) in task A and answer these questions.

a According to the principles you have been looking at in this session, in what ways is the text *cohesive*?
b In what ways is it *coherent*?
c What kind of text (or *genre*) does it belong to (if any)?

15 Presenting the meaning and form of new grammar items

A Warm-up

1 Imagine you are trying to learn to use new computer software. Do you prefer:
- to be told how to do it?
- to be shown how to do it?
- to read how to do it?
- to try using it and find out for yourself?
- a combination of these?

2 How is your knowledge of how to use the computer software likely to change over time?

3 Would you learn the grammar of another language following the same principles as you would to learn a new computer program? Why / Why not?

B Presenting grammar from texts

1 Look at this text-based presentation – Sections A–C. Answer the questions (a–d) that follow.

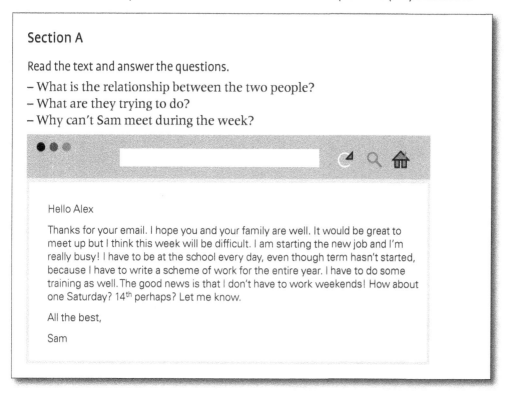

Section A

Read the text and answer the questions.
– What is the relationship between the two people?
– What are they trying to do?
– Why can't Sam meet during the week?

Hello Alex

Thanks for your email. I hope you and your family are well. It would be great to meet up but I think this week will be difficult. I am starting the new job and I'm really busy! I have to be at the school every day, even though term hasn't started, because I have to write a scheme of work for the entire year. I have to do some training as well. The good news is that I don't have to work weekends! How about one Saturday? 14th perhaps? Let me know.

All the best,

Sam

Section B

Look at this sentence from the text: *I have to be at the school every day.* Underline other examples of *have to* in the text.

Complete the rules:

Have to is followed by a verb in the i_____e form. *I have to get up early.*

We use *have to* + *infinitive* to show o_____n.

Don't have to + *infinitive* is used to show that there is a c_____e – there is no o_____n.

Section C

Write four sentences using *(don't) have to* about yourself.

a What are the advantages of using a text to contextualize new language items?
b What happens before the focus on the grammar item?
c How is this grammar item presented in this example?
d What happens after the focus on the grammar item?

2 When using texts to present language items, which of the following statements offer good advice? Cross out any that offer poor advice.

a The text should have several examples of the target form.
b The text should provide enough data from which 'rules' can be worked out.
c The text should be long and complicated.
d The context should be recognisable and easily comprehensible.
e The text should provide clues to the meaning of the new item.
f Only written texts should be used.
g The text should sound reasonably natural.

C Three more presentation techniques

1 Complete the table after each presentation. Study the first one in the box below.

Presentation technique 1 – Using the learners' first language

[After the students have read a text]

Teacher: Spójrz na dwa zdania z tekstu. [Teacher writes two sentences on the board.]

She has worked in Barcelona for three years. She worked in the UK before that.

Teacher: Gdzie ona jest teraz? [Students answer.]

Teacher: Jaka jest różnica między dwiema formami czasownika? [Students answer.]

Teacher: Używaj *have* i *past participle* do opisywania sytuacji, które się nie skończyły. Jak to się mówi po polsku? [Students answer.] Czym różni się gramatyka (polska) od gramatyki angielskiej? [Students answer. / Teacher explains.]

Teacher: Teraz zajrzyj do książki. Uzupełnij zdania odpowiednią formą czasownika. [Students open their books.]

Which structure or structures are presented?	
How is the new language item (or items) contextualized?	
What are the advantages of using the learners' first language at this stage?	
What are the disadvantages?	

Presentation 2

Your trainer will demonstrate a technique for presenting new language.

Which structure or structures are presented?	
Choose one: – the teacher principally explains the item – the teacher creates a situation from which to highlight the item – the teacher uses a text to highlight the item	
What are the advantages of this technique?	
What are the disadvantages?	

Presentation 3

Your trainer will demonstrate another technique for presenting new language.

Which structure or structures are presented?	
Choose one: – the teacher principally explains the item – the teacher creates a situation from which to highlight the item – the teacher uses a text to highlight the item	
What are the advantages of this technique?	
What are the disadvantages?	

2 Look back at tasks B and C. Answer the questions.

  i Which two presentation techniques does the teacher have most control over?

  ii Which presentation technique is most learner-centred?

  iii Which presentation technique is least learner-centred?

  iv Which technique(s) would you most enjoy as a learner?

D Presenting new language items and highlighting form

1 Here is one simple sequence for presenting new language items.

1 The teacher provides and/or elicits some meaningful model sentences which use the target form.
2 Where necessary, the teacher focuses on the pronunciation of the new item.
3 The teacher writes some examples of the intended item on the board.
4 The teacher highlights the key features of the new language from the examples on the board.
5 The teacher writes the form on the board, matching it to the examples.
6 The teacher checks that the learners understand the meaning of the form.

Match the stages (1–6, above) with what the teacher says or writes on the board (a–f, below).

1 _____ 2 _____ 3 _____ 4 _____ 5 _____ 6 _____

a On the board:

> Monika has run a marathon.
> Chico has been on television.
> We have all studied languages!

b On the board:

> Monika has run a marathon.
> Chico has been on television.
> We have all studied languages!

has/have + past participle

c On the board:

> Monika has run a marathon.
> Chico has been on television.
> We have all studied languages!

d The teacher says:

> Look at the sentence: Monika has run a marathon.
> Is she running a marathon now?
> Did she run a marathon in the past?
> Do we know exactly when she ran a marathon?
> [Students answer the questions.]

e The teacher says:

> Listen to this sentence: Monika has run a marathon.
> Where's the stress in the sentence? How does it sound? Listen again …

f   The teacher and the students have a conversation:

Teacher: Today we are going to talk about interesting things we have done in our lives –
something unusual. For example, what do you think I have done?
[Shows picture of bungee jump.]

Student 1: You do crazy jump.

Teacher: That's right – we call it a bungee jump. How do you think I felt?

Student 2: Frightened.

Teacher: No, not frightened … . *Very* frightened. Now think about the grammar. What verb
do we use for my experience? I have …

Student 1: Did – no, done. Did.

Teacher: Which one?

Student 1: Done.

Teacher: Good. I have done a bungee jump. Now tell me about you.

Student 3: I have ranned a marathon.

Teacher: Wow – really? That's amazing. Where was that?

Student 3: In my country – in Gdansk and Gdynia.

Teacher: Well done! Amazing. But not ranned, – run. Can you say it? I have run a
marathon.

Student 3: I have run a marathon.

2   This is one way of presenting language. In a lesson, what would come after the presentation phase?

3   In (f), the teacher elicits example sentences from the students by creating a situation in which they talk
about experiences. How else could a teacher contextualize the language?

E   Putting it into practice

1   Your trainer will give you a new item of language to teach. Talk to your partners and discuss how you
could do it in *two* different ways. Remember, you need to:

- use examples
- make the meaning clear
- highlight the spoken form
- highlight the written form

2   Present the language item to the class, using one of the techniques you talked about.

KEY WORDS FOR TEACHERS

Check you know the meanings of these terms.

- *contextualization*
- *form*
- *meaning*
- *highlighting (form)*
- *model sentence*
- *target form*
- *structure*
- *presentation*

REFLECTION

Look back at what you have done in this unit. Look at the following statements and complete the table by putting each in either the DOs or DON'Ts columns. When you are ready, compare your answers with a partner. Can you add any other statements to the table?

- Check that learners have understood the meaning.
- Give a lecture about grammar.
- Involve learners in the process as much as possible.
- Where possible, draw comparisons and contrasts between English and the learners' own language(s).
- Always use the same presentation technique.
- Contextualize new language items (e.g. by using a reading or listening text).
- Use clear examples.
- Highlight the form.
- Make explanations clear and concise.
- After presenting new language items, give plenty of opportunities for learners to use the language.

Presenting new language items	
DOs	DON'Ts

Translation for Presentation 1 Task C

[After the students have read a text]

T: Look at these two sentences from the text.

She has worked in Barcelona for three years. She worked in the UK before that.

T: Where is she now? [Students answer.]

T: What's the difference in the verb form? [Students answer.]

T: So, use *have* and a past participle for something that hasn't finished. How do we say that in Polish? [Students answer.] How is the grammar different to English? [Students answer. / Teacher explains.]

T: Now, look in your books. Complete the sentences with the correct verb form.

16 Checking the meaning of grammar items

A Warm-up

1 Match the first part of the sentence (1–6) with an appropriate ending (a–f).

1 If I were you, I would try to	a when you explain new language items.
2 My advice would be to give the learners	b both the spoken and written form of new language items.
3 Why don't you start with the speaking	c keep explanations of new language quite brief.
4 In your position, I would try to involve	d as much time as possible to use the new language.
5 You should use examples	e the learners as much as possible.
6 Make sure that the learners know	f activity to see what learners already know?

2 Answer the questions.

   a Which language function do all the examples fulfil?
   b Which phrases could be used in a formal situation?
   c Are there any phrases that would usually only be used to give advice in an informal situation?
   d Do you agree with the advice given on teaching new language items? Is there any of the advice that you would like to clarify with your trainer?
   e Could you use this type of matching activity in your teaching? If so, for what purpose(s) could it be used?

B Checking understanding

A teacher is teaching *used to + infinitive*, using *She used to live in Athens* as an example sentence.

1 What is the key concept conveyed by *used to + infinitive*?

2 Which of the questions a–d is a useful check of the learners' understanding of the concept?

   a Do you understand?
   b Did she use to live in Athens?
   c How do you say that in your language?
   d Did she live in Athens in the past? Does she live there now?

> Checking understanding of vocabulary, using similar techniques, is dealt with in unit 7 Task E.

Compare your ideas with a partner.

3 Work in pairs. Write questions to check the understanding of the structures in bold. Start by identifying the key concept you wish to check. (Assume that the learners understand the individual words.)

   a They **are flying** to New York tomorrow (the present continuous used for a future plan/arrangement).
   b When I arrived at the cafe, Alex **had left**.
   c **If I were** Prime Minister, **I would give** everyone more holidays.

C Timelines

Timelines are simple diagrams that can help learners to see relationships between verb forms and their time reference. This diagram illustrates the sentence *I'm reading a book at the moment.* Notice that the line starts 'before now' and continues 'beyond now'. Here, the wavy line is used to indicate the temporariness implied in the sentence.

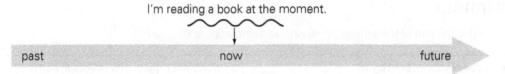

There is no one correct way to draw timelines, but learners need to know the conventions you are using.

1 Match the sentences with the timelines.

  a She used to ride a motorbike.
  b She used to live in Athens.
  c I'm living in Australia at the moment.
  d I get up at 6.30 every morning.

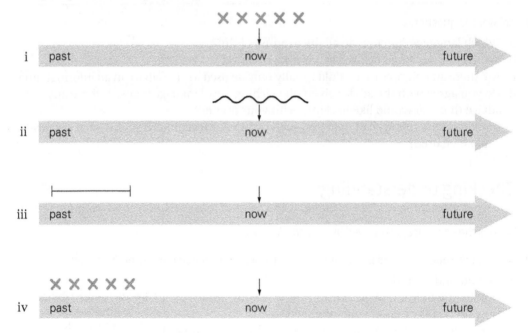

2 Draw timelines for the following sentences.

  a The business will have closed down by the end of the year.
  b I've been working there for ages.
  c When I arrived at the cafe, Alex had left.

When you are ready, show your drawings to a partner and see if they can match them to the sentences.

D Analysing material

1   Look at the material below and answer the questions that follow.

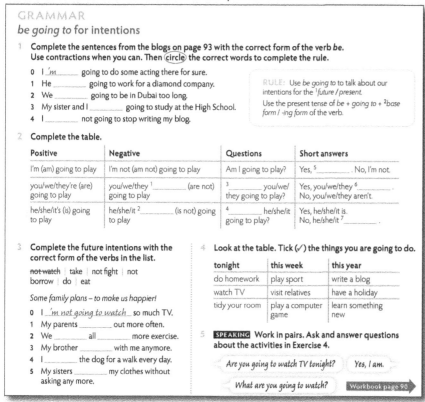

GRAMMAR

be going to for intentions

1   Complete the sentences from the blogs on page 93 with the correct form of the verb *be*.
    Use contractions when you can. Then (circle) the correct words to complete the rule.

    0   I _'m_____ going to do some acting there for sure.
    1   He _____ going to work for a diamond company.
    2   We _____ going to be in Dubai too long.
    3   My sister and I _____ going to study at the High School.
    4   I _____ not going to stop writing my blog.

    > RULE: Use *be going to* to talk about our intentions for the [1]*future / present*.
    > Use the present tense of *be* + *going to* + [2]*base form / -ing form* of the verb.

2   Complete the table.

Positive	Negative	Questions	Short answers
I'm (am) going to play	I'm not (am not) going to play	Am I going to play?	Yes, [5]_____ . No, I'm not.
you/we/they're (are) going to play	you/we/they [1]_____ (are not) going to play	[3]_____ you/we/ they going to play?	Yes, you/we/they [6]_____ . No, you/we/they aren't.
he/she/it's (is) going to play	he/she/it [2]_____ (is not) going to play	[4]_____ he/she/it going to play?	Yes, he/she/it is. No, he/she/it [7]_____ .

3   Complete the future intentions with the correct form of the verbs in the list.

    ~~not watch~~ | take | not fight | not borrow | do | eat

    Some family plans – to make us happier!

    0   I _'m not going to watch_ so much TV.
    1   My parents _____ out more often.
    2   We _____ all _____ more exercise.
    3   My brother _____ with me anymore.
    4   I _____ the dog for a walk every day.
    5   My sisters _____ my clothes without asking any more.

4   Look at the table. Tick (✓) the things you are going to do.

tonight	this week	this year
do homework	play sport	write a blog
watch TV	visit relatives	have a holiday
tidy your room	play a computer game	learn something new

5   **SPEAKING** Work in pairs. Ask and answer questions about the activities in Exercise 4.

    > *Are you going to watch TV tonight?*   *Yes, I am.*

    > *What are you going to watch?*   Workbook page 90

Think 1

1   The sentences in section 1 come from texts that the learners have just read, so the learners have already seen these examples. Why is this desirable?

2   How have the materials writers ensured that the sentence completion in exercise 1 will be quick and simple to complete for most learners? Why is it beneficial for example sentences to be easy to complete?

3   How are the rules about form and use conveyed to the learners?

4   What is the purpose of exercise 2?

5   What is the purpose of exercise 3?

6   How does exercise 4 relate to exercise 5?

7   How is the practice in section 5 different to the practice in exercise 3?

8   How can exercise 5 be made as communicative as possible?

9   What would you expect the teacher to do during and after exercise 5?

10 Do you like the sequence of the material? Would it be appropriate for a class you are currently teaching?

2   Read these comments from teachers about using the material above. Suggest a rationale for why each teacher made the changes they did.

    1   I missed out exercise 1 and instead told my students what they needed to know, and then they completed exercise 2 and the rest of the sequence.

2 I added an activity after exercise 2: I gave the students three sentences in English to translate into Spanish and then three in Spanish to translate into English.

3 I typed out exercise 2 in much bigger font and with more spacing for two of the students in the class.

4 I added some options to exercise 4, things like 'cook a meal' and 'help my mum' – things I know some of my students have to do. I gave them time to ask me for any vocabulary they needed.

5 I always put some of the specialized words that books use – contraction, infinitive and so on – on the walls of the classroom, so that the learners know what I am talking about!

KEY WORDS FOR TEACHERS

Check you know the meanings of these terms.

- *form*
- *meaning*
- *concept-checking question*
- *timeline*
- *personalization*
- *differentiation*

REFLECTION

Answer the questions.

One-star questions

a Describe, as if to an elementary learner, the verb form in this sentence: *They didn't leave until nearly midnight.*
 b Look at this sentence: *If I found a wallet in a taxi, I would give it to the police.* Which of the following questions is **not** useful for checking understanding?
    i Does this refer to the past?
    ii Is it likely I will find a wallet in a taxi?
    iii If you found a wallet, would you give it to the police?
 c Think of two reasons why a teacher might decide to use the learners' first language when teaching grammar.

Three-star questions

a Look back at the material in task D.
    i How could you make the presentation of the language easier for learners?
    ii Think of at least one way in which you could make the material more challenging for the learners.
 b Imagine you have taught the present perfect simple using the example sentence *They've lived in the same house for as long as I can remember.*
    i Underline the present perfect simple elements of the sentence.
    ii Think of a question you could use to check learner understanding.
    iii Draw a timeline that would be appropriate for this sentence.

Five-star question
Look ahead to a lesson you will teach in the future where there is a focus on vocabulary, language functions or grammar. i How will you convey the meaning of the new items? ii How will you convey the form of the new items? iii How will you check understanding? iv Do the learners have opportunities to practise the new items? Are the practice opportunities sufficient? v Is there anything you need, or want, to change about the material?

17 Practising new language items

A Warm-up

Read the following texts and answer the question. Share your ideas with a partner.

1 Do you think that either of these experiences compares to the experience of learning a language? For example, what is the role of practice?

> I remember having tennis lessons. We would spend ages just practising one shot – hitting backhands over and over again, or volleying at the net, or whatever. My coach was trying to make that one piece of my game perfect. The lessons would always finish with a short match, though, where I had to use all the shots I could play – that was probably the bit I liked best.

> For me, being a chef is just my dream job – I love cooking so much. I would always go into the kitchen when my mum was cooking and I watched everything she did. She then let me start to help – chopping stuff up, that sort of thing. And then one day I just said, 'I'll cook this' – and she watched me do it all. If I got something wrong, she'd gently tell me, but it was really just all me. When I started, nothing was quite as good as she would have done, but I just kept cooking things and learning as I went along.

2 Read the quote below. In your own experience of learning a second language, was practice useful? If so, what kinds of practice were helpful?

> Practice gets a raw deal in the field of applied linguistics … For some, the word conjures up images of mind-numbing drills in the sweatshops of foreign language learning, while for others it means fun and games to appease students on Friday afternoon. Practice is by no means a dirty word in other domains of human endeavour, however. Parents make their kids practise their piano skills at home, and the world's most famous performers of classical music often practise for many hours a day, even if it makes their fingers hurt. If even idolised, spoiled, and highly paid celebrities are willing to put up with practice, why not language learners, teachers, or researchers?
>
> Robert DeKeyser, 2007

B Controlled oral practice

1 Look at the lesson transcript below and answer the questions that follow.

Teacher:	Listen. She's been to Spain. She's been to Spain. Now you. Repeat.
Class:	She's been to Spain.
Teacher:	Good. Again.
Class:	She's been to Spain.
Teacher:	Good. Cinzia, can you say it?
Cinzia:	She has been to Spain.

Teacher: OK – but put 'she' and 'has' together – 'she's'.
Cinzia: She's been to Spain.
Teacher: Excellent. Roberto ...

a What are the advantages of this type of repetition exercise?
b What are the drawbacks?
c Why might the teacher choose to start with choral repetition (the whole class responding)?
d Do all new language items need to be drilled?
e Do all learners in the class need to say the new item individually?

2 Look at an alternative drilling technique below – known as 'backchaining'. What is the purpose
   of backchaining?

Teacher: Listen. She's been to Spain. Repeat after me – to Spain.
Class: to Spain.
Teacher: been to Spain.
Class: been to Spain.
Teacher: She's been to Spain.
Class: She's been to Spain.

3 Work with a partner to practise backchaining. Trainee A should use model sentence A, with trainee B
   responding, and trainee B should use sentence B.

A: I'm going to paint the house in the summer.
B: We'll call you when we arrive.

Controlled written practice

1 Read exercises a–c and explain how they differ.

---

a Complete the sentences with the words in the box.

applied	bought	finished	invited	messaged	went

1 I .... to the supermarket yesterday and .... some bread, coffee and pizzas.
2 Paula .... me yesterday and .... me out to dinner.
3 She .... the course and .... for a job in LA.

---

b Complete the sentences with the correct form of the words in the box.

apply	buy	finish	go	invite	message

1 I .... to the supermarket yesterday and .... some bread, coffee and pizzas.
2 Paula .... me yesterday and .... me out to dinner.
3 She .... the course and .... for a job in LA.

---

c Complete the sentences by putting one word in each gap.

1 I .... to the supermarket yesterday and .... some bread, coffee and pizzas.

2 Paula .... me yesterday and .... me out to dinner.

3 She .... the course and .... for a job in LA.

---

2 Explain how these practice exercises are different from drills. What advantages do you think they have? What can you conclude about providing practice?

D Interactive and communicative practice

1 Read the activities and complete the chart that follows by ticking the appropriate boxes.

A. Dialogue practice (to practise the past simple)

---

1 In pairs the learners practise the following dialogue:

A: Hello Pat, did you have a nice weekend?

B.   Yes. I went *skiing*.

A: That sounds like fun. What was the weather like?

B: It was fantastic. What about you? What did you do?

A: I stayed at home. We had a *barbecue*.

B: Was that fun?

A: It was until *I burned myself!*

2 They change the elements in italics to make a new dialogue, and practise that.

B. Circle drill (to practise the present perfect)

The learners sit in a circle. The teacher shows the first picture (the Eiffel Tower) to a learner and asks, *Have you ever been to France?*. The learner answers; the teacher gives the picture to the learner who turns to the next learner and asks the same question and then passes the picture on. The teacher then continues with the other pictures, so that all the pictures are travelling around the circle with the learners asking and answering questions.

C. **Find someone who ... (to practise *can*)**

Learners stand up and mingle, asking questions so as to find people who can do the different activities. They then report back to the class.

> FIND SOMEONE WHO ...
>
> can swim
>
> can speak more than three languages
>
> can juggle
>
> can play the piano
>
> can sing
>
> can drive a car

D. **Write five sentences (to practise the present simple)**

The learners must write three true sentences about themselves, using the new item of language (in this case the present simple) and two which are not true. They read their sentences to a partner, who must guess which are true.

	Dialogue practice	Circle drill	Find someone who ...	Write five sentences
There is built-in repetition: the activity gives learners opportunities to use the new language item on several occasions.				
The language is contextualized.				
Learners interact and/or take turns.				
Learners communicate – they must both speak and listen to what is said.				
The language is personalized.				
The activity is fun and playful.				

2 Choose two of the criteria from the left-hand column and say why these things are useful in a practice activity.

3 Work in pairs. Write two exercises to practise *used to* + base form, as in *He used to do magic tricks*. Which sequence would you recommend the activities be used in? Why?

E Putting it together

Think back to what you know about presenting new language items, as well as how to provide practice. Work in pairs. Complete the lesson plan, using the boxes a–j below.

1 Below is part of a lesson plan on using *used to* + base form to express past habits. Try to complete the plan, matching the boxes a–j below with boxes 1–10 in the plan.

Lesson aim: Expressing past habits with *used to* + base form.

Stage	Activity
Building context	1
2	Teacher says, *David used to play football.*
Highlight meaning	3
4	Teacher asks, *Did he play football in the past?* (Yes) 'Does he play football now?' (No)
Highlight spoken form	5
6	The teacher writes the model sentence on the board. Draws a box round *used to* and writes *base form* over *play*.
Summarize 'rule'	7
8	Learners choose an activity they enjoyed as children and then walk round the class asking if other people used to do the same thing.
Report back	9
10	The learners discuss their memories of their first school in small groups.
Report back	The teacher asks some individuals what they talked about. Afterwards, she highlights good uses of language and writes some errors she heard on the board and asks learners to correct them.

a	The teacher draws a timeline on the board, showing a period in the past with several crosses within it.
b	The teacher repeats the model sentence with natural linking, stress and intonation. The class repeats.
c	Highlight written form
d	The teacher asks some individuals how many people shared their interest and corrects errors if they are made, as well as praising good examples of language use.
e	The class talks about what things they enjoyed doing when they were children.
f	Teacher says, *used to + infinitive can be used to talk about things we regularly did in the past, but don't do now.*
g	Practice 2
h	Model sentence
i	Practice 1
j	Checking understanding

Check you know the meanings of these terms.

- *controlled (restricted) practice*
- *choral repetition*
- *individual repetition*
- *drill*
- *interaction*
- *communication*

REFLECTION

Think about the following questions. When you are ready, work in groups and discuss your answers.

1 Why do learners need to practise language if they already know the 'rules'?
2 How would you respond if learners made errors in the sort of activities you have seen in this unit?
3 As well as the sort of practice activities you have seen in this unit, what other types of practice activity would you need for a balanced lesson?
4 Is there a correct order for sequencing practice activities? What factors might influence a teacher's decision as to which practice activities to use, and when?

Reference

DeKeyser, R. (2007) *Practice in a Second Language: Perspectives From Applied Linguistics and Cognitive Psychology.* Cambridge: Cambridge University Press.

18 Providing feedback on learner production

A Warm-up

1 Decide which of these teachers' views you agree with. Then work in groups and compare your ideas.

Olga:

> Errors need to be avoided at all costs. I don't want my learners to pick up bad habits.

Mariagrazia:

> Errors are a natural part of the learning process – and as teaching material they're really useful.

Paula:

> I feel bad correcting my students' errors – it's judgemental and demotivating.

Tomas:

> I think it is really important that teachers highlight good examples of language use, because it builds the confidence of the student who said it and other students can learn by copying it.

Carol:

> I think it is really important to praise learners' effort and perseverance, as well as when they get something 'right'.

Marco:

> I try to involve my students in correction. Sometimes they can correct themselves, or another student can correct them.

2 Think back to your own language learning experience. Did you like it when the teacher corrected your errors? Why / Why not? Did your teacher highlight good examples of language use?

Compare your experiences with a partner.

> Many language teachers and students believe the provision of negative feedback by the teacher in speaking and writing is a staple of good classroom instruction.
>
> Lourdes Ortega, 2009

B Types of error

1 Find the errors in the sentences (1–6) and match them with the classifications (a–f). Then compare your answers with a partner.

Errors	Classification
1 She likes her job. She works for the same company for years.	a problem with word stress
2 (In a restaurant) Bring me the menu!	b problem with intonation
3 My brother fell off his bike but he wasn't badly damaged.	c problem with word order
4 It's a lovely day, isn't it?	d problem with choice of word(s) (vocabulary)
5 She's a MATure student.	e problem with register
6 Where is standing the teacher?	f problem with the choice of verb form

2 Think about some of the errors your learners have made in teaching practice. Do the errors fit one of the types above, or are they different?

C When to intervene

Work with a partner. Look at some options teachers have for giving feedback. Read the situations below and discuss which you would use in each situation. Be ready to justify your choices.

> correct immediately   delay correction until the end of the activity
> ignore the error   praise immediately   praise after the activity

1 You are monitoring group work and you hear learners in different groups say these things:

  a 'Technology is such important for all of us these days.'
  b 'For sure, I am agree with Anja.'
  c 'Salma makes a brilliant point.'
  d 'The battery is terrible – I have to redo it every hour!'

2 The following exchanges occur on different occasions in open class:

  a You: We have a new student today. Welcome Vera! Vera, can you introduce yourself?
     Vera: I am coming from Moscow. I am absolutely happy to join this class.

  b You: Monika, can you tell us what your group talked about?
     Monika: We think that endangered species need safe habitats.

  c You: Freddie, tell us about your job.
     Freddie: I work in hotel. My job is to make the guests.

3 The following exchanges happen in open class as learners report back their answers to a listening exercise:

  a You: What instrument does he play?
     Student: He is play saxophone.

  b You: What did she say about her favourite movie?
     Student: She doesn't like black and white movies.

D Correction strategies

1 Work in pairs. Compare the ways that different teachers responded to the same error. Explain the strengths of each strategy and identify any potential disadvantages. Complete the table below.

Learner:

'We go to the beach yesterday.'

Teacher 4:

Sorry, do you mean you go every day?

Teacher 1:

Yesterday – so, grammar?

Teacher 5:

You went to the beach – that's nice. Who did you go with?

Teacher 2:

Yesterday you …

Teacher 3:

Not quite; look: We go to the beach yesterday.
[Holds up their hand and indicates the second finger from the left from the learners' point of view]

Teacher 6:

[makes no comment and the activity continues until, at the end, the teacher says] I heard someone say *We go to the beach yesterday*. Can anyone correct that?

Strategy	Advantages	Disadvantages
Teacher prompts using terminology – e.g. 'grammar, tense, pronunciation,' etc.	Easy to use and prompts the learner to self-correct. Indicates the type of error that the learner should be looking for.	Learners need to be familiar with the terminology used.
Teacher repeats the utterance to the point of the error. e.g. *Yesterday you …*		
Finger correction (teacher uses fingers to indicate the position of the error)		
Teacher asks a question to establish the meaning, e.g. *Do you mean you go every day?*		
Reformulation (recast), e.g. *You went to the beach.*		
Delayed correction		

2 Think about lessons you have observed. Did the teacher use any of the strategies shown here? If so, were they effective?

E Putting it into practice

1 Read out the error on the card you are given and respond to what your trainer does or says. Pay attention to how the trainer corrects the error.

2 Look at the list of errors and complete the table.

Error	How was it corrected?
Can you borrow me some money?	
Do you can juggle?	
Bring me the menu!	
Where is going Felipe?	
Her mother is a PROfessor.	
My brother fell off his bike but he wasn't badly damaged.	

3 Can you think of any alternatives that could have been used to correct these errors?

4 Work in a group of three. Your trainer will give you a set of cards. Each card has an error on it.

Trainee A: Play the role of the learner. Take a card and read out the error.
Trainee B: Play the role of the teacher. Correct A's error.
Trainee C: Play the role of an observer. Give feedback on the success of the correction strategy.

Take turns playing each role.

KEY WORDS FOR TEACHERS

Check you know the meanings of these terms.

- *feedback*
- *immediate correction*
- *delayed correction*
- *reformulation*
- *peer correction*

REFLECTION

1 Use the prompts below to write sentences about giving feedback. The first one has been done as an example.

1. there are/types *There are different types of error.*
2. learners/expect
3. correction/quickly
4. correction/clearly
5. immediately / interfere with meaning

6. sometimes/delayed/because
7. no fixed rules / when or how
8. praise/sincere
9. praise/effort
10. feedback/supportive

2   Do you agree with all the advice given in the sentences above?

3   Read the quote below. Explain how errors 'invite opportunities'.

> Feedback is most effective when students do not have proficiency or mastery – and thus it thrives when there is error or incomplete knowing and understanding … Errors invite opportunities. They should not be seen as embarrassments, signs of failure, or something to be avoided. They are exciting, because they indicate a tension between what we *now* know and what we *could* know.
>
> John Hattie, 2012

References

Hattie, J. (2012). *Visible Learning for Teachers*. London: Routledge, p.139.

Ortega, L. (2009). *Understanding Second Language Acquisition*. London: Hodder Education, p.72.

19 Teaching language items reactively

A Warm-up

1 Look at this definition of *reactively*.

> reactively (adverb): in a way that reacts to events or situations, rather than acting first to change or prevent something.

Cambridge Dictionary

What do you think that *teaching reactively* means? How do you think it might differ from teaching pre-selected items?

2 Read the sentences below. Put a tick next to any you definitely agree with. Put a cross next to those you definitely disagree with. Put a question mark against any that you are unsure about.

- Teaching reactively means putting learners first.
- Teaching reactively means never using a coursebook.
- Teaching reactively means never planning lessons.
- Teaching reactively starts with a focus on meaning.
- Teaching reactively is only for experienced teachers.
- Teaching reactively involves setting up an activity, monitoring and giving feedback.

Work with a partner and explain your choices.

> I harness the communication, because I can't control it, and base my method on it.
>
> Sylvia Ashton-Warner, 1963

B Planning a reactive lesson

1 a Number the lesson stages below so that they form a logical sequence.

☐ The learners work in small groups to complete the activity.

☐ The learners report back what they discussed.

☐ The teacher monitors the groups carefully – listening and writing down examples of good language use and also areas of possible improvement.

☐ The teacher shows an interest in what the learners say, praises and highlights good uses of language and elicits, or shows, how the learners' use of language could be improved.

☐ The teacher sets up a group speaking activity.

b What happens between the learners finishing the group activity and the teacher providing feedback on the language they used to communicate?

2 Put the phrases below into the correct box to summarize this approach to teaching.

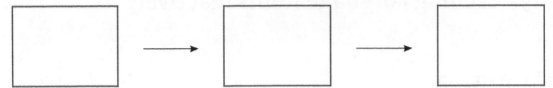

monitor and support learners
give feedback
set up and encourage communication

3 How might a teacher scaffold (or support) the learners' output during monitoring?

4 After completing the stages in 2, above, a teacher decides to set the same, or a very similar, activity to the one they used in activity 1. Think of advantages of doing this.

C Selecting what to teach

1 One of the challenges of teaching reactively is to select appropriate language items on which to focus from the learners' output. Teachers need to monitor activities carefully to be able to do this.

Look at the notes below, made by a teacher during group work. The learners were sharing information in order to solve a murder mystery puzzle.

Good points	Things to correct/improve
They must've got in through the window. (Good pronunciation, good grammar)	X There are four suspect (/suːspekt/). X
How many suspects are there? (Good vocabulary)	X They must had know each other. X
Sorry, I interrupted. After you. (Very polite!)	X The window broke and the glasses is all over the floor. X
There is a fingerprint. (Good vocabulary)	X Does the police interview the business partner? X
	X The victim he goes to the police now. X
	– Where is the document that has the information about who will have money of the dead one?
	– There were three persons in the house, I think.

Work in small groups. Take turns to select one of the notes from either column and explain to your partners how you would use it in the feedback stage of the lesson. For example:

- Would you write anything on the board?
- What questions would you ask?
- What information would you give?

2 Here is an extract from the discussion of one group in the same lesson. Work in small groups. Pick out some things that you would highlight as good examples of language use. Pick out some things to correct/improve.

Ateeqa:	I think the reason is for the money.
Jonas:	Yeah, right. I am agree with you. Kah Yee, what do you think?
Kah Yee:	I think the cooker might be the guilty. He has argued with the victim.
Ateeqa:	Oh yeah, I forgot that. But the cook isn't working that night.
Jonas:	I think the cook is not the person we need.
Kah Yee:	Let's repeat what we know for sure.
Jonas:	Good idea. Ateeqa, what you said?
Ateeqa:	Before?
Jonas:	Yes.
Ateeqa:	OK. I think the reason is the money. They all need money!
Kah Yee:	The business partner wanted to sell the business. I think that is importance.

3 Work with another group. Take turns to choose an item from your list in activity 2 and use it to 'teach' the other group.

D Concerns of teachers

Look at the comments on teaching reactively from teachers. Can you give advice to help any of these teachers?

Teacher 1:

I can't always hear what the students are saying, and I feel I have let the students down if I don't comment on anything they said.

Teacher 2:

I would like to teach by responding to what students say, but I am worried that I won't be able to explain their mistakes if I don't prepare before the lesson.

Teacher 3:

I tried this with a class of 20 students and it was a bit chaotic. Most of the students chatted in their own language.

Teacher 4:

I have seen this type of teaching work really well. But at my school there's a fixed syllabus and we are expected to work from that.

Teacher 5:

I think my students expect a fairly traditional grammar lesson. I'm worried that they will think that they are not learning anything.

Teacher 6:

What about practice? How can I give the students any practice when I teach them something new?

Teacher 7:

I worry that the cycle of communication followed by correction can become repetitive.

KEY WORDS FOR TEACHERS

Check you know the meanings of these terms.

- *teaching reactively*
- *preselection*
- *(giving) feedback*
- *monitoring*
- *scaffolding*

REFLECTION

Think about answers to these questions. When you are ready, compare your ideas with a partner.

1 Does every lesson need to have a pre-selected grammar point?
2 What would you say to someone who said: 'I don't like reactive teaching. Students need to learn grammar.'?
3 Can you summarize how teaching reactively is different to other ways of presenting new language?
4 Can you think of any circumstances where teaching reactively might be particularly appropriate?
5 Have you tried teaching reactively? Would you like to?

Reference

Ashton-Warner, S. (1963). *Teacher*. London: Virago.

20 Focus on listening skills

A Warm-up

1   Write a list of all the things you listened to in the last 24 hours. For example:
    - listening to a podcast while at the gym
    - ordering a takeaway coffee at a café

    Compare your list with a partner.

2   Decide which of your 'listening experiences':
    a   involved you speaking as well as listening, i.e. which were *interactive,* as opposed to those which were 'one-way', i.e. *non-interactive*
    b   was supported by visual information, either verbal (e.g. written text) or non-verbal (e.g. pictures)
    c   involved listening to a speaker who was physically present
    d   involved listening for specific information
    e   required you to listen closely and attentively
    f   allowed a less attentive style of listening

3   What difficulties might learners have with each of these listening events?
    - watching a live lecture
    - watching a recorded version of the lecture
    - listening to a podcast of the lecture on headphones
    - listening to a recording of the lecture in a classroom
    - discussing the lecture with a colleague, face-to-face
    - talking about the lecture with colleagues in a live-streamed conference call

B Comprehension

1   Listen to your trainer reading two (unrelated) texts. After you have listened, answer these questions.
    1   Did you understand all the words in the text?
    2   Did you understand the overall meaning of the text?

2   Now listen again, and answer these questions.
    1   What was different about each text, the second time you heard it? Were the texts easier to understand?
    2   What factors make comprehension easier or more difficult?
    3   What are the implications of this activity on listening and reading in the classroom?

C Listening texts and tasks

1   Match each listening text type (1–9) with appropriate tasks (a–l). There may be several tasks that are suitable for each text type.

Listening text types	Listening tasks
1 a news broadcast	a answering *wh*-questions (*where, who, what, why?* etc.)
2 an exercise routine	b putting a series of pictures in order
3 the directions to a local landmark	c ticking off items on a list of names of people and places
4 the description of a missing person	d drawing on a map
5 an embarrassing personal anecdote	e filling in a grid or table
6 a shopping dialogue (sales assistant and customer)	f choosing one of several pictures
7 a pop song	g taking notes
8 recorded timetable information	h choosing one of several adjectives
9 a weather forecast	i writing the exact words
	j drawing a picture
	k filling in gaps in a transcript
	l performing actions

2   Compare ideas with a partner. Explain your criteria for choosing tasks.

D A listening lesson

1 Read the coursebook extract and identify the purpose of each of the activities marked with an arrow (→).

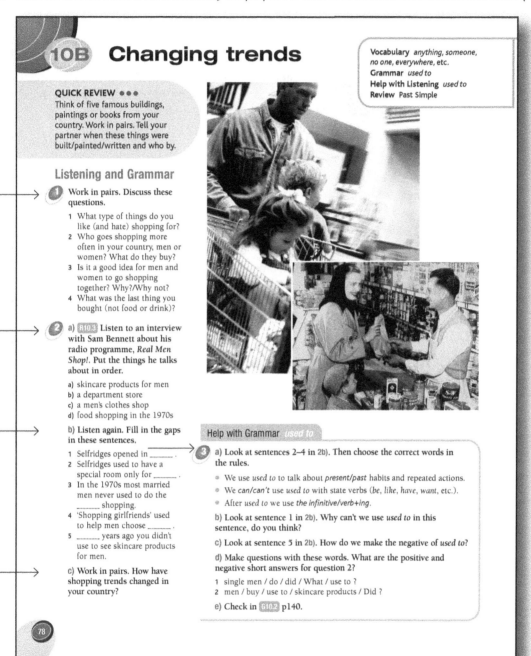

face2face Pre-intermediate

2 How could you adapt this sequence:

   1 to make it easier for students with less developed listening skills?
   2 for an online class?

3 Put these stages of a listening task into a logical order.

  a The teacher focuses on features of grammar or vocabulary that occur in the recording, e.g. by asking students to complete the gaps in a transcript.

  b The teacher sets a task that requires listening for specific details. She plays the complete recording, checks the task, and replays sections if necessary, addressing issues (such as barely audible words) that may be causing problems in understanding.

  c Learners read the transcript of the recording and listen at the same time.

  d The teacher generates interest in the topic by, for example, asking the class about their experience of, feelings about, or knowledge of, the topic.

  e The teacher presents some key vocabulary in the listening text, e.g. by giving, or eliciting, a definition or an example.

  f Learners are invited to respond to the text, e.g. based on their own experience of the topic.

  g The teacher sets a gist listening task, e.g. *Who is talking to whom, about what, and why?* She then plays a short section of the recorded extract, and checks the answers.

4 Explain the principles underlying your choice of order. For example:

- Learners will listen with more attention if their interest has been aroused (d).

E Classroom application

1 Put the stages in activity D3 in the correct column.

Pre-listening tasks	While-listening tasks	Post-listening tasks

2 Work in groups. Design a sequence of tasks for the following recorded text (in which people are talking about their jobs) that you could use with a group of pre-intermediate students. Include at least one pre-listening task, one or more while-listening tasks, and one post-listening task.

NIGEL:	I became a pilot about 20 years ago. I had to do 72 weeks' basic training, but I didn't have to pay for it – the company did. I was lucky, I suppose, and now I have a job that I love. But these days most pilots have to pay a lot of money to do their training.
GARY:	You don't have to go to university, but you probably learn more facts than a university student – at least that's what people say! A London taxi driver has to know 25,000 streets and all the important places in the city.
MELISSA:	It's not easy to become a vet. You have to have a degree and the training takes five years. And you don't have much free time when you're a student vet – you have to work very hard.

face2face Pre-intermediate

Check you know the meanings of these terms.

- *interactive/non-interactive listening*
- *(listening for) gist*
- *intensive listening*
- *pre-/while-/post-listening tasks*

REFLECTION

Read the questions and suggest some answers.

Questions about listening, posted by teachers on an online discussion forum.

Q1: How important IS listening? My students just want to speak.

Q2: My students hate listening to recordings. Is there an acceptable alternative, such as reading the transcripts to them aloud?

Q3: When I do a listening activity in class, the students get frustrated if they can't understand every word. How can I discourage them from trying to do this?

Q4: My students say that they like listening to songs, but I'm not sure that this is a good idea. Should I let them, and, if so, is there an effective way of using songs?

Q5: Many coursebook listening texts sound a bit stilted and unnatural. Is there a good reason for this, and is there a viable alternative?

Q6: My students complain that they can understand recordings in the classroom, but that they have problems understanding real people when they talk to them. How can I help them with this?

21 Focus on reading skills

A Warm-up

Here are some statements about reading. To what extent do you agree? Discuss these statements in pairs or groups.

a Reading means knowing how to sound out the letters in words.
b Comprehension means understanding all the words in a text.
c Reading, in the classroom, means reading aloud.
d For teaching purposes, texts should be simplified.
e Reading is a good way of improving vocabulary.
f If you can read well in your first language, you should be able to read well in a second one.

B Reading purposes and strategies

1 Identify the reasons for reading, and the ways of reading, for these different text types:

Text type	Reason for reading		Way of reading		
	primarily for pleasure	primarily for information	close (intensive) reading	skimming for gist	scanning for specific information
instructions for playing a board game		✓			
a memo from your boss					
a weather forecast					
the news report of a sports event					
a short story					
a research paper published in a scholarly journal					

C Reading in a second language

1a   Look at this text (in Esperanto) and answer the questions.

1   What kind of text do you think it is?
2   What is it about?
3   How are these names connected: Tonto, Andreo, Betty?
4   How does the story end – happily or unhappily?

KATO RETROVIS SIAN FAMILION POST 4.000 KILOMETRA VOJAĜO

Kato, kiu vojaĝis 4.000 kilometrojn, revenis al siaj posedantoj, kiuj kredis, ke ĝi estis mortinta. La kato, Tonto, malaperis kiam ĝiaj posedantoj, kiuj loĝas en Hamilton, Ontario, feriis en Vankuvero. La tagon, kiam ili devis reveni hejmen, ili ne sukcesis trovi la katon. Andreo kaj Betty Overden ne havis alian elekton ol lasi Tonton al lia sorto. Mirakle Tonto ekkomencis la 4.000-kilometran vojaĝon trans Kanado. Li bezonis nur 3 semajnojn por alveni hejmen. 'Mi ne povis kredi miajn okulojn', diris Betty kiam la kato aperis unu matenon en ŝia ĝardeno en Hamilton. 'Tonto sidis tie, malsata kaj malpura, sed vere feliĉa revidi nin!'

---

b   Read the text again and try to answer the questions (also in Esperanto).

1   Kiel nomiĝas la kato?
2   Kiom da kilometroj vojaĝis la kato?
3   Kiom da semajnoj li bezonis?
4   Kie Betty trovis sian katon?

2   Compare ideas with a partner.

1   How many questions (in parts 1a and 1b) could you answer? What clues were you using in order to answer them?
2   Rate your comprehension of the text on a scale from 0 to 10.
3   What does this tell you about reading in a second language?
4   What can the teacher do to help learners understand a text like the one above?

D Coursebook reading texts and tasks

1 a Identify the purpose of the tasks 1, 2a, 2b, 3a and 3b in this coursebook extract. Decide if they are pre-reading, while-reading or post-reading tasks.

b Why do you think some sections of the text are in bold type?

9A ▶ Get healthy!

Vocabulary health
Grammar relative clauses with *who, that, which, whose, where* and *when*

QUICK REVIEW Warnings and advice
Imagine a friend from the UK is coming to live and work in your town/city. Think of five warnings or pieces of advice to give your friend. Work in pairs. Compare sentences. What's the most important warning or piece of advice?

Reading and Listening

1 Work in groups. Discuss these questions.

1 Do you think you have a healthy diet? Why?/Why not?
2 How often do you eat things that you know are bad for you?
3 Has your diet changed since you were a child? If so, how?

2 a Before you read, check these words with your teacher or in a dictionary.

| a fast | go on a retreat | toxins | digest |

b Read the article. Did the journalist feel healthier after doing the retreat? Why?/Why not?

3 a Read the article again. Tick the true sentences. Correct the false ones.

1 You only drink vegetable juice on the retreat.
2 Joanne wasn't looking forward to the experience.
3 Louise worked at the retreat centre.
4 Fasting helps your body get rid of toxins.
5 Joanne felt fine on day two of the retreat.
6 The fifth day was easier than the third day.
7 Joanne has changed her diet since the retreat.

b Work in pairs. Discuss these questions.

1 Would you like to go on a retreat like the one in the article? Why?/Why not?
2 Do you know anyone who has been on a retreat like this? If so, did they enjoy it? Why?/Why not?

Just Juice

Can giving up food really improve your health?
Joanne Fullerton spent a week at a retreat centre to find out.

When I arrived at the Just Juice Retreat Centre, I was feeling a bit nervous. I was going to do a seven-day fast, drinking only fresh organic fruit and vegetable juices. I'm the type of person **¹that eats three meals a day** and can't wake up without a cappuccino, so the idea of living on juice for a week was rather terrifying.

After checking in, I was taken to the guest house **²where everyone was staying**. Louise, the woman **³who I was sharing a room with**, had been on the retreat four times and she looked healthier than anyone I'd ever met. According to Rachel Carr-Hill, the woman **⁴whose fasting programme we were following**, going without food is one of the best things we can do for our health. The food **⁵that we usually eat** contains toxins **⁶which stay in our bodies** and stop our digestive system working properly. When we fast, our body doesn't have to digest food, so it has time to get rid of these toxins.

The first day started with yoga at seven o'clock and then we had 'breakfast' – a big glass of carrot juice. We spent the day listening to talks about health, having massages and relaxing, with a different juice meal every three hours. On the second day I had an awful headache and felt as if I was getting a cold. Apparently this was a normal reaction because my body was starting to get rid of the toxins. On day three my headache was much worse and this was also **⁷when I started getting really hungry**. I began daydreaming about cheeseburgers, pasta, chocolate – anything but more juice. However, by day five the hunger had gone and I felt more relaxed than I'd been for years. At the end of the retreat I'd lost three kilos and felt like a new woman. Now I'm much more careful about what I eat – but I still can't live without my morning cappuccinos!

face2face Intermediate

2 Work in groups. Imagine that you are going to use the following text with a group of intermediate learners.

a Decide which features might help understanding and which might make it difficult to understand.

b Design at least one *pre-reading,* one *while-reading,* and one *post-reading* task to use with this text

Then compare ideas with another group.

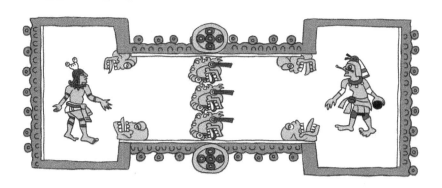

Pok-a-tok:
THE MEXICAN BALL GAME

From ancient times a ritual ball game was played by all the peoples of Mexico and Central America. The ruins of almost every ancient city include a walled court that was used for this sacred game. In Mexico alone, well over 600 stone ball courts have been found.

The game (called *pok-a-tok* by the Aztecs) is no longer played and the rules were never written down. What we know about it is based on drawings and on descriptions by the first European visitors. Apparently, the players were divided into two teams. Each team fought for possession of the ball. On either side of the rectangular court were two long sloping walls. The object of the game was to drive the ball through rings that were positioned on these walls. The ball was solid rubber, probably a little larger than a modern basketball, and would have weighed several kilos. The rings were almost identical in diameter to the balls, which must have made it extremely difficult to score. It seems that the first team to score won.

The players were not allowed to hit the ball with their hands or feet. They could use only their knees, hips and elbows. The ball could not touch the ground. Ballplayers used cotton pads and thick leather clothing to protect themselves from the ball. Evidently, players were often injured, despite these protective measures. The game seems to have had a religious significance. It may have been a re-enactment of an ancient creation myth. Perhaps the ball symbolized the sun as it moved from the east to the west across the sky. If played correctly, the game would cause the sun to shine, the rain to come at the right time, and the crops to grow.

E A reading lesson

1   Put these stages of a reading lesson in a logical order. (There may be more than one order).

   a   Check detailed understanding by asking true/false questions.
   b   Focus on vocabulary in the text by asking learners to find words that mean X, Y, Z.
   c   Use a picture or some discussion questions to generate interest in the topic.
   d   Ask learners to read the text quickly in order to answer gist questions, e.g. *What's it about? Who wrote it? Why?* and then check their answers.
   e   Ask learners to talk about their personal response to the text and its topic.
   f   Teach essential vocabulary that learners may be unfamiliar with.
   g   Focus on a grammar structure in the text by, for example, asking learners to underline each instance of it.
   h   Use the title of the text to encourage students to predict the content of the text.

2   Choose a reading text in a coursebook that you are using. Identify any *pre-, while-* and *post-reading* tasks. Using ideas from the previous activity, could you add anything to the sequence of tasks?

KEY WORDS FOR TEACHERS

Check you know the meanings of these terms.

- *skimming*
- *scanning*
- *comprehension*
- *bottom-up/top-down knowledge*
- *reading for gist*
- *intensive reading*
- *extensive reading*
- *reading strategies*

REFLECTION

Discuss these questions.

a   What is the advantage of choosing reading texts that are accompanied by illustrations, diagrams or maps?
b   What are the pros and cons of using real (i.e. authentic) texts, rather than texts that have been specially written or adapted for classroom purposes?
c   Why is setting a task in advance of reading a good idea?
d   What does 'matching the task to the text' mean? (If in doubt, refer to Task B above). Why is it a good idea?
e   Why is it often a good idea to let students compare their answers to reading comprehension questions?
f   Should learners be allowed to consult dictionaries and/or translation apps while reading? What is the alternative?
g   Should learners answer comprehension questions from memory, or should they be allowed to consult the text? Why / Why not?

22 Focus on speaking skills

A Warm-up

1   Look at the questions below and think about how you would answer them. When you are ready, discuss them in small groups.

1   What languages (other than your own) can you speak?
2   In your experiences as a language learner, how much did you speak in lessons? Did you enjoy lessons that focused on speaking?
3   What skills and knowledge does someone need to be able to speak a language?
4   What makes speaking a language other than your own difficult?

2   Report back your discussions to the class.

> 'Speaking' is so much part of daily life that we take it for granted. However, learning speaking, whether in a first or other language, involves developing subtle and detailed knowledge about why, how and when to communicate …
>
> Burns and Seidlhofer, 2020

B Speaking activities

1   Like writing, speaking is both an important skill in its own right, and also a vehicle for practising new language items. Look at the four activities below. For each, say whether the emphasis is on speaking for communication, or language practice.

1   The teacher shows pictures of famous places around the world. The learners respond with *I have(n't) been to Rome,* etc.
2   The teacher asks the learners about the places that they would most like to visit and why. The learners respond.
3   The learners work in small groups to compare their ideal jobs.
4   The learners work in small groups to compare their answers to a grammar exercise.

2   The following activities focus on speaking for communication. Which of the following five activity types have you experienced as a learner? Which did you enjoy?

Discussion activity

The activity in A above is an example of a discussion activity. Of course, for learners of English the questions could be changed so that there is a focus on a topic of interest to the learners.

Role play

Look at the scenario on the next page. Your teacher will allocate you one of the roles. Take a few minutes to think about your role and plan the arguments you wish to put forward.
There will be a meeting between the headteacher at a school, a teacher at the school and a student representative.

Role: Headteacher You are new to the school and want to show that you listen to students' views. On the other hand, you do not want to upset your staff. You will chair the meeting.

Role: Teacher You believe that mobile phones are being used excessively in lessons. They stop students focusing on the lesson and it is clear that many students are using social media rather than studying. You think mobile phones should be banned in the classroom. Put your arguments forward at the meeting.

Role: Student representative You represent your class. You know that one or two students use their phones for social media in lessons but most of them are using phones to check facts and find additional information relevant to the lesson. Put the case for using mobile phones in lessons at the meeting.

Conversation

The teacher begins by asking the learners their views on a topical issue of interest. The teacher encourages the learners to ask, as well as answer, questions. They may address these to the teacher or other learners. As the conversation develops, so other topics might be introduced.

Information gap

An activity type where the information required to complete the task is distributed across two or more learners, meaning that they must communicate in order to complete the task successfully. See the Unit 34 task on pages 181 and 183 for an example.

Survey and presentation

1 In groups of four, prepare a survey on the topic: *Are you a good language learner?* Prepare six questions that you will ask the other students in the class. For example: *Do you do the homework that the teacher gives us?* a always   b sometimes   c never
2 Form new groups, so that each student in the new group comes from one of the original groups. Ask the other students your questions, and make a note of their answers.
3 Return to your original group. Share the results of your survey. Prepare a presentation of your findings. Use expressions like *Five out of ten students always do their homework*. Draw some conclusions from your survey. For example, *It would be good if we could listen to more songs in English. This would improve our listening skills ...*
4 Present your findings and conclusions to the class.

3 Look at the five different activity types above again. For each activity type, answer the following questions.

a Could it be used with classes at a range of levels?
b Could it be used with a range of class types and sizes?
c Is there a purpose to the activity? Is there an outcome?
d Could it be used in both online and face-to-face lessons?

4 Look again at the activities and answer the following questions.

   a Which activities encourage learners to share personal information and opinions?

   b Which activities could be set up so that the grammar and vocabulary required by the learners can be predicted by the teacher, and even pre-taught if necessary?

   c What would the teacher's role be before, during and after these activities?

C Giving advice: concerns of learners

Look at these comments from learners on speaking lessons. What advice could you give to them and/or their teachers?

1 'We do some speaking in class, but it is dominated by a few students and some of us don't say anything.'

2 'I get very anxious that when I try to use English no one will understand me.'

3 'I'm in a B2 class and I can speak OK, so speaking in class is a bit of a waste of time.'

4 'Speaking is so important for me and I want to practise outside class, but don't know how.'

D Giving advice: concerns of teachers

Look at these comments from teachers on speaking lessons. What advice could you give to them?

1 'I know I should correct mistakes, but I sometimes have trouble hearing the students when they work in pairs and so I don't know what to correct.'

2 'When I use breakout rooms I worry. I can't be in every room and so I don't know what learners are doing.'

3 'I am afraid of using too much pair and group work because the students sometimes use their own language.'

4 'The book I am using has some interesting speaking activities, but I cannot find a grammar point to link to them.'

KEY WORDS FOR TEACHERS

Check you know the meanings of these terms.

- *information gap*
- *role play*
- *monitoring*
- *outcome*
- *speaking for communication*

> **REFLECTION**
>
> Work with a partner from another TP group. Look at the books that you are using with your respective groups and choose one speaking activity from each. For the purposes of this activity, ensure that it focuses on speaking for communication, as opposed to solely practising a particular language point. Consider the following questions.
>
> 1 Do you like the material? Would you be happy to use it with the appropriate group?
> 2 Choose one of the pieces of material. How could you make it maximally productive? For example, how could you ensure that as many learners as possible are speaking as much of the time as possible?
> 3 Write the stages you would go through in order to exploit the material. Would you adapt the material in any way?
> 4 As the teacher, what would you need to do before, during and after the activities?

Reference

Burns, A. and Seidlhofer, B. (2020). Speaking and Pronunciation. In N. Schmitt and M. Rodgers (eds.), *An Introduction to Applied Linguistics* (3rd edition). Abingdon: Routledge.

23 Focus on writing skills

A Warm-up

Look at the following comments made by practising teachers. Which views do you agree with? Discuss your ideas in small groups.

Tracy:

I sometimes think that writing in class is a bit of a waste of time. The learners can do it at home and we have so many other things to fit into lessons anyway.

Korali:

I use writing in class to give learners the chance to produce grammatically accurate sentences.

Chris:

I like to teach writing by showing the students an example of the sort of text they should write. We talk about the structure of the text, and then they write a similar text.

Laura:

I make sure my learners know how to use spell checks and grammar checking software, as well as where they can find online dictionaries. I am in two minds about how much I should encourage the use of machine translation – I think it is inevitable that people will use it.

David:

I don't think you should correct every mistake when learners write something. I only pick out what I think are the main points, and I always write comments saying what I liked about what was said, or what I thought was surprising, and so on.

Quyen:

I like to get my students to comment on each other's written work, because I think they can learn a lot from that.

B Writing activities

1 Look at the activities below and complete the table.

a Multiple choice gap-fill
   The learners choose the best way to complete sentences. For example:
   We had a nice holiday, _____ the weather was bad.

a) despite	b) despite of	c) because	d) although

b Reproducing a model
   Learners study a model text and then write their own text of a similar nature. For example, they read an email of complaint and answer questions about the layout of the email and the content of each paragraph; afterwards they write their own email of complaint.

c Interactive writing
   Learners interact in writing. For example, they write text messages to each other and respond.

d Writing an essay
  Learners write an essay. For example, they discuss the achievements of a famous person.

e Dialogue writing + items
  Learners write a dialogue that includes preselected language items. For example, they must include five words that are given by the teacher.

Analysis of activity types					
Activity type	Is there a communicative purpose?	Do the learners produce texts?	Is the activity similar to what learners might do outside the language classroom?	Does the writer know who the reader will be?	What level could it be used for?
a Multiple choice gap-fill					
b Reproducing a model					
c Interactive writing					
d Writing an essay					
e Dialogue writing + items					

2 Work in small groups. Look at the following writing task and answer the questions.

> Write six sentences describing your favourite film.

a How could you make this exercise more communicative?

b How could you redesign it so that learners produced a single, unified text, rather than a list of sentences?

c How could you make it more authentic?

d How could you provide a readership?

C Stages in writing

1 Imagine writing a blog post about a particular teaching context with which you are familiar. Put the stages below in the order in which you would do them. Are there any things here that you wouldn't do?

a Write a final copy.

b Read and make changes and corrections.

c Write a rough draft.

d Organize ideas.

e Consult books and/or talk to colleagues to get ideas.

2 We can see from C1 above, that writing involves a number of different processes. In small groups, discuss the implications this has for teaching.

D Providing feedback on written work

Work in pairs. Discuss the three ways in which the errors in this learner writing have been indicated and answer the questions.

1 Which of the three ways do you think is most effective?
2 The writer of the text was at intermediate level (B1). Do you think the approach to correction would be the same for all levels?
3 What do the symbols mean? Complete the key.

> Response to student writing, or 'feedback', is one of the most important – and time-consuming – activities undertaken by any writing instructor.
>
> Dana Ferris, 2018

As you know, this product _is_ on sale for four years and we want_increase _sale_. We have some ideas for _advertise_ the product. Healthy products are fash_i_nable now and we should _to_ focus on this.

Our product is ~~make~~ **made** from herbs and we can ~~to~~ tell people this. One of the idea'_s_ is to ~~changed~~ the name because now it is difficult to ~~pronunciate~~ **pronounce**. Also we ~~belief~~ **believe** that we need|**to** update the ~~wraps~~ **wrapper**.

Also, we are deciding the price should _T_ cheaper than _G_ competitors _becuase_ _+_ we can _do_ _sp_ more market _ww_ share this way. In addition _P_ we should _to_ _un_ be an official sponsor at the next Olympic Games. But television _publicity_ _ww_ is also very important.

ww = wrong word   wo =   T =   un =
sp = spelling   G =   P =   + =

E Analysing material

Look at the material aimed at A2 level learners. It is taken from a section in the coursebook called 'Skills for Writing'. In the previous section, the learners listened to a recording of a student discussing which homestay family he should choose when he goes to study in Australia.

Answer the questions.

1 What is the overall purpose of 2a and 2b?
2 What is the overall purpose of 3a, b and c?
3 What is the overall purpose of 4a, b and c?
4 What is the purpose of exercise 4d?
5 What is the purpose of exercise 4e?
6 Could you use this material with the learners you are currently teaching? Would you want to adapt it in any way?
7 How could you make the task at 4d more challenging for stronger learners?
8 How could you make the task at 4d less challenging for weaker learners?

2 READING

a Ahmed decided to stay with the Conways. Read his email to them. Tick (✓) the main reason he writes to them.

1 ☐ to ask about their house
2 ☐ to tell them about all the sports he likes
3 ☐ to tell them about himself
4 ☐ to explain how much he wants to study

b Read the email again. Number the information in the order you find it.

☐ his future plans ☐ his hobbies
☐ his family's jobs ☐ his hometown

Dubai

Dear Mr and Mrs Conway

My name is Ahmed Al Mansouri and I come from Dubai in the United Arab Emirates. Thank you for offering to be my homestay family when I'm in Sydney.

I am 23 years old and study biology at university. I live with my family in Dubai. My father is a businessman and my mother is a doctor. I've got one brother and one sister. They're university students too.

In my free time, I like playing football (I think you say 'soccer' in Australia!) and meeting my friends. I like watching different kinds of sports with them.

While I'm in Sydney, I really want to study hard and improve my English because I want to become a marine biologist after I finish university. I'd really like to work in a country like Australia.

I'm looking forward to meeting you when I arrive.

Best wishes

Ahmed

Dubai

3 WRITING SKILLS
Linking ideas with *after, when* and *while*

a <u>Underline</u> the word in each sentence that's different from Ahmed's email.

1 Thank you for offering to be my homestay family while I'm in Sydney.
2 I want to become a marine biologist when I finish university.
3 I'm looking forward to meeting you after I arrive.
4 When I'm in Sydney, I really want to study hard.

b Look at the sentences in 3a and complete the rules with the words in the box.

after   beginning   while

1 We use *when* and _____ to join two activities that happen at the same time.
2 We use *when* and _____ to join two activities that happen at different times.
3 If the linking word is at the _____ of the sentence, we use a comma (,) between the two parts.

c <u>Underline</u> the correct words. There is more than one possible answer.

1 *After / When / While* I finish my English course, I'd like to go to Canada for a holiday.
2 I'd like to go skiing in the mountains *after / when / while* I'm on holiday.
3 I often play basketball with my colleagues *after / when / while* I finish work.
4 *After / When / While* I watch a game of football, I usually want to play a game myself.
5 My English improved *after / when / while* I was in Sydney.

4 SPEAKING AND WRITING

a Make a list of English-speaking countries you know.

b 💬 Which country in 4a would you like to visit? Why?

I'd like to go to …

I like warm places.

They say the people are friendly.

c Plan an email about yourself to a homestay family in that country. Make notes about:
- your age
- study / job
- what you'd like to do in that country
- free-time interests
- family

d Write your email. Tick (✓) each box.

☐ Start the letter with *Dear*
☐ Say thank you
☐ Say who you are
☐ Talk about study / work / free time
☐ Talk about your family
☐ Say what you want to do in the country
☐ Include *I'm looking forward …*
☐ Finish the letter with *Best wishes*
☐ Use *after, when* and *while* to link your ideas

e 💬 Swap emails with another student and check the ideas in 4d.

77

Empower A2

Check you know the meanings of these terms.

- *process*
- *readership*
- *purpose*
- *corrective feedback*
- *authentic task*

REFLECTION

Complete the following sentence in as many different ways as you can. Try to use one of the words in the box below in each sentence you write.

collaborative	communicate	grammar	model texts	process writing	readership

To teach writing ...

Reference

Ferris, D. (2018). Writing instruction and Assessment. In J. Newton, D. Ferris, C. Goh, W, Grabe, F, Stoller and L. Vandergrift (eds.), *Teaching English to Second Language Learners in Academic Contexts.* New York: Routledge.

24 Teaching basic literacy

A Warm-up

Read the definition of literacy and answer the questions.

> Literacy is the ability to read and write in a language – usually one's own – and is contrasted with illiteracy, or the state of being illiterate. [...]
>
> However, increasingly for learners of a second language – especially those living in an English as a second language (ESL) context – the term 'literacy' is used to mean more than simply reading and writing as an end in itself, but reading and writing as a means to assimilate into the target language community and its culture.
>
> Scott Thornbury, 2017

1 What typical reading and writing tasks face a new arrival to an English-speaking country? For example, understanding and filling in a form to register with a doctor.
2 Why might doing reading and writing in a typical general English class be unlikely to meet the special needs of such learners?

B L1 and L2 literacy

Read the learner profiles and answer the questions.

> Aasmah moved to Australia from Afghanistan nearly three years ago. She has picked up a fair amount of spoken language but has never had formal lessons. She cannot read or write any English but has a good command of writing in Farsi, her first language.

> Halima moved to Canada from Somalia. She works in Canada and listens and speaks well. However, she cannot read or write any English, and she never had the opportunity to learn to read or write in her own language either.

> Huseyin is an electronics engineer and a recent arrival in the UK from Iraq. He is literate in both Kurdish and Arabic, and speaks English fluently. He can read and write English sentences but cannot handle the kinds of documents that he needs in order to apply for a job, rent a flat, or get a driving licence, for example.

1 To what extent is each learner literate or illiterate in: a) their first language(s); b) English?
2 Why would it be difficult to comment on the overall level of English possessed by each learner?
3 Consider the ways in which most learners are taught new vocabulary and grammar. Why might Aasmah and Halima find learning these things harder than some classmates?
4 What skills, if any, do you think Aasmah and Huseyin may be able to transfer from reading and writing in their first language(s) to reading and writing in English?
5 Why do you think the ability to read and write sentences is insufficient for Huseyin's needs?
6 What else does Huseyin need to know about reading and writing in English to be able to confidently do the things he needs to?

C Lessons from learners

1 Read what these learners say about learning to read and/or write in English. In each case write what you should remember when you teach basic literacy. Then compare your answers with a partner.

Learner	Comment	I should remember …
Karim	I always get very anxious before reading things in class. It's quite intimidating. It helps if there is not too much on the page and if the writing is quite big.	
Soula	I was very lucky with my teacher. She gave me lots of time to find the letters on the keyboard. She never got frustrated with me and always encouraged me.	
Li Na	It was a bit frustrating. The teacher kept practising letters and sounds. Eventually we went on to words. And then sentences. It was months before I read a little story. I wanted to move on.	
Shireen	It's very frustrating if you are trying to learn to read but you don't actually understand the words anyway – they are all new.	
Vashti	I know the alphabet, but the teacher keeps using different fonts or asking us to read other learners' handwriting. Outside class it's often hard for me to read signs because they're all in capital letters and the shape of the words are all the same.	
Ali	The worst thing is that it is just so tiring. I concentrate so much I get tired and then my writing gets worse.	
Samia	My teacher always said 'copy this from the board' — new words, grammar, those things — but I never had time. I felt I missed out and fell behind the other students, but I was worried about seeming stupid if I asked the teacher to wait for me.	
Daryan	My handwriting was very bad – the teacher couldn't read what I was writing. I found it so difficult. But then a teacher helped me and showed me how to hold the pen and now I'm improving a little.	
Mei Yan	Some people in my class can read and write quite well. They write quickly but for me, if I copy things, I can't remember more than one or two letters at a time. It's very difficult.	
Shan	I never write by hand. It's much easier to type. I use predictive text, a spell checker or a translator if I can, but I don't always know if it's correct. I can also ask my phone to read texts to me, so I don't have to read them myself.	

2 All of the learners described so far are neurotypical adults. The areas you discussed in C1 may also be important to consider if you teach pre-literate young learners or learners with Special Educational Needs (SEN), such as dyslexia, dysgraphia or deafness. Write YL and/or SEN next to each point in the table which you think is relevant to these learners too. Then compare your answers with a partner.

D Reading activities

Work in pairs. Put these reading activities into the correct column.

Activities focusing on reading at word level	Activities focusing on reading at sentence level	Activities focusing on reading at text level

a Reading bingo
The teacher gives out bingo cards with known vocabulary on them. She reads out items of vocabulary. The winner is the first person to tick off all the words.

b Find and underline
The teacher gives out a short text about eating habits. The learners must underline all the types of food mentioned.

c Odd one out
The learners see a set of words. They have to say which word is the odd one out. For example, *March, April, Tuesday, June*.

d Matching
The teacher creates flashcards or an online game with pictures of known vocabulary and the corresponding words. The learners must match the pictures to the appropriate word.

e Ordering
The teacher gives out a short text but the sentences are in the wrong order. The learners must put the text into the correct order.

f Describing pictures
Learners read a series of sentences and choose the correct picture in each case. For example, there are two pictures, one of a set of keys on a table, and one with keys on a chair. The learners read 'My keys are on the table' and must select the correct picture.

g Next word
The teacher gives out a short text. The teacher begins to read the text to the class, but every now and then stops and asks, *What is the next word?*.

h Sentence halves
Learners see the first half of a sentence. They must select the correct second half from a list.

E Writing activities

Three writing sub-skills important in basic literacy are spelling, the mechanical formation of letters (i.e. how to move a pen to create a letter on a page), and writing simple sentences. Find two activities that practise each of these sub-skills from the following list:

a The teacher gives out a handout on which there are pictures of known vocabulary. Scattered around each picture are the letters to make the written form and a space underneath for the form to be written.

b The letters of the alphabet are printed on a piece of paper in the form of a series of dots. The learners must join the dots to form the letters.

c The learners are given a model sentence. The learners must write a similar sentence of their own. The first word is given.

Ania is from Poland.

I ....

d The teacher displays a sentence where all of the words run together and there is no punctuation. Learners must rewrite the sentence with the correct spaces and add relevant punctuation. For example, *imfrombaghdadiniraq*.

e The teacher writes simple words on pieces of paper in thick pen. She gives one to each learner. The learners place another piece of paper over this and then trace the word onto their own piece of paper.

f The teacher selects eight items of vocabulary each week and teaches the written form. Every day the learners must read the words, and then cover them and try to write them out correctly.

KEY WORDS FOR TEACHERS

Check you know the meanings of these terms.

- *literacy*
- *special educational needs (SEN)*

REFLECTION

Work in groups. Complete the diagram below.

Our tips for teaching literacy

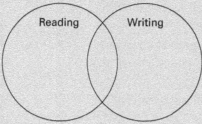

Reading   Writing

Reference

Thornbury, S. (2017). *A New A–Z of ELT*, Macmillan, p.160.

25 Integrating skills

A Warm-up

1 Your trainer will give you an activity to do. Work with a partner to complete the activity.

2 Answer the questions.

   a What skills (speaking, listening, reading and writing) did you personally practise in this activity?
   b What skills did your partner practise?
   c Did you enjoy the activity?
   d Would you be able to use this type of activity with a class you are teaching?
   e Could the activity be used in both virtual classrooms and physical classrooms?
   f According to the text, why is it a good idea to combine skills in the classroom?

> ... we should be looking for opportunities to knit skills together, because this is what happens in real life.
>
> Donn Byrne, 1976

B Combining skills

1 Look at the following activities. Work in groups. Tick the skills that you think would be involved in each one.

	Listening	Speaking	Reading	Writing
a Learners do a 15-minute role play in pairs. Half the class are journalists, who interview the other half of the class, who are environmental campaigners.				
b Learners work briefly in small groups to discuss ideas to put into a piece of writing on animal rights. They then do a piece of writing in the style of a blog post on the subject.				
c Learners read a text about language teaching methodologies and answer multiple-choice questions. They discuss their answers in small groups before reporting back to the teacher.				
d Learners read a short description of a podcast. They then listen to the podcast and answer some true/false questions.				
e Learners work in pairs to write a review of a restaurant they like.				
f Learners make notes as they listen to a short, pre-recorded lecture.				

2 In the above table, choose one of the four skills and look at the activities (a–f) it occurs in. Is it equally central to the activity in each case? What implications might this have for teaching?

3 Choose a combination of two skills that you feel learners in your TP group would benefit from practising more. Look at the coursebook you are using in teaching practice. Choose some activities that you think would include the two skills you have chosen, and consider the balance of the skills in the activities. Are the skills equally prominent in all cases?

C How teachers combine skills

1 Look at the comments made by teachers on how they combine skills in lessons. Complete each one with a word or phrase from the box.

communicative	give feedback	model text	nodding and asking
read a text	speaking and listening	the transcript	to discuss

a A lot of my writing lessons include reading, because the learners study a _____ before they write.

b Most of my reading lessons contain some speaking and listening because I ask learners _____ their reactions to the text.

c Speaking lessons must include listening or they cannot really be called _____ .

d As learners often talk to each other in lessons, I try to teach active listening skills near the start of the course, such as _____ questions.

e In so-called speaking lessons, I also sometimes _____ on how well the learners have used active listening techniques.

f In some of my listening lessons, we study _____ to highlight features of spoken language. This means that the learners also do some reading, and also their speaking may improve.

g I sometimes _____ aloud to my learners and they follow it. This helps them read more quickly and, of course, includes listening practice.

h My writing lessons often contain _____, because I ask learners to share ideas before they write.

2 Respond to the prompts below.

a Choose one thing from the exercise above that you already do.

b Is there anything from the exercise above that you think you could incorporate into your own teaching?

c Share your ideas with your partner.

D Putting it into practice

Here is a text about an approach to teaching called Content and Language Integrated Learning (CLIL). Think of different ways the text could be exploited so that all four language skills are practised. You can use different activities to practise different combinations of skills.

One way in which skills are very naturally integrated in language teaching is in *content and language integrated learning* (CLIL). This is when the teacher teaches a school subject – such as mathematics or science – *through* the target language (such as English). The aim is to develop both subject knowledge and language skills at the same time. This may result in a teacher deliberately teaching particular items of vocabulary or grammar in order to support learners in understanding and producing the texts that are relevant to the subject area.

KEY WORDS FOR TEACHERS

Key words for teachers

Check you know the meanings of these terms.

- *integrated skills*
- *active listening*
- *CLIL*
- *receptive skills*
- *productive skills*

REFLECTION

Play in groups of three or four. Each player needs a counter and should place it on the start line. Players flip a coin. If the coin lands on 'heads' they move one square, and if it lands on 'tails' they move two squares. When a player lands on a square s/he should answer the question to the satisfaction of the other player(s). If s/he does not answer to the satisfaction of the other player(s), s/he must go back to the square s/he moved from.

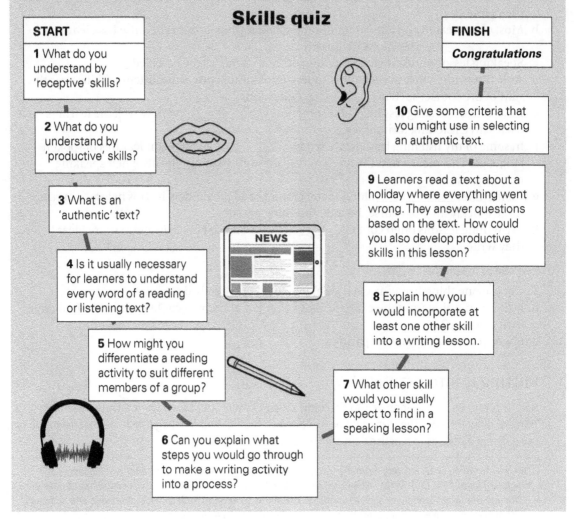

Skills quiz

START

1 What do you understand by 'receptive' skills?

2 What do you understand by 'productive' skills?

3 What is an 'authentic' text?

4 Is it usually necessary for learners to understand every word of a reading or listening text?

5 How might you differentiate a reading activity to suit different members of a group?

6 Can you explain what steps you would go through to make a writing activity into a process?

7 What other skill would you usually expect to find in a speaking lesson?

8 Explain how you would incorporate at least one other skill into a writing lesson.

9 Learners read a text about a holiday where everything went wrong. They answer questions based on the text. How could you also develop productive skills in this lesson?

10 Give some criteria that you might use in selecting an authentic text.

FINISH

Congratulations

Reference

Byrne, D. (1976). *Teaching Oral English*. London: Longman.

26 Lesson planning: defining aims

A Warm-up

1 Choose the statement(s) you agree with. Discuss your choices with a partner and agree on an order of importance.

Lesson aims are important because …

a trainers (and directors of studies) require them.
b they make planning easier.
c they make lesson plans look more professional.
d they frame the criteria by which the lesson will be judged.
e learners need to know the focus of the lesson.
f they set a goal that can be used to test the learners' achievement.

2 Look at the quote from Amy Tsui. What sort of knowledge about students do you think that expert teachers might use when planning? Discuss your ideas with a partner.

> Expert teachers always start their lesson planning with their knowledge of the students. Novice teachers, however, tend to focus on what they want to do as a teacher and give relatively little attention to how students will respond to their teaching.
>
> Amy Tsui, 2009

B Types of aim

1 Look at the following five lesson aims. Four of them relate to the same lesson. Which one do you think is the odd one out?

a To present and practise the form and use of the present perfect with *ever* and *never*.
b By the end of the lesson, the learners will have talked about and compared past experiences.
c By the end of the lesson, the learners will be able to express future plans and arrangements.
d The learners will take part in informal conversation.
e To develop my grammar presentation skills.

2 Match the lesson aims (a–e) in activity B1 with the types of aim in the box below.

communicative aim (× 2)	professional developmental aim
linguistic aim	skills aim

3 Choose the most appropriate aim (a–f) for the lesson described by the teacher below. What is unsatisfactory about the other aims?

a to do some speaking
b to present and practise the past tense
c to practise writing
d the learners will tell each other stories about disastrous holidays
e to develop oral fluency when narrating past events
f by the end of the lesson, the learners will have learned some new words

> *I'm going to start by telling the students about a recent holiday I had which was a bit of a disaster, and this will involve some past tense examples. Then I'm going to get them to work in pairs to reconstruct my story in writing, and I'll check that they've used the same verbs correctly. Then I'll ask them to think of their own stories, about trips or holidays where things went wrong, and to prepare to tell these stories to each other. To do this they'll first need to plan their stories, and they can use translating apps to look up any words they need. Then I'll put them in pairs to tell their stories. After that, I'll change the pairs so they can tell their stories again, to someone different. This way they can get more fluent, hopefully.*

4 Read the lesson descriptions A and B, below.

a Identify each teacher's main aim and at least one subsidiary aim.
b Formulate each teacher's aims (both main and subsidiary), using the rubric: *By the end of the lesson …*
c State whether the main aim is linguistic, communicative, or skills-focused.

A.
> *I've got a short text about a driving instructor. So the students are going to read that and answer a couple of comprehension questions. I've chosen the text because there are lots of examples of the present perfect simple and continuous. So the text is a way of contextualizing the language so that we can contrast the verb forms and then do a bit of practice.*

B.
> *We are going to start by talking about money and what students spend their money on. I'm then going to teach verbs that combine with money, like earn money, save, lend, borrow, invest money and so on. I'll then share a profile of a person with financial trouble and the students will write a plan for them of how to improve their financial situation, using some of the verbs I've taught them.*

Material and aims

1 For each of the two following pieces of coursebook material, identify and formulate:

a a main aim
b a possible subsidiary aim

2 Classify the aims that you have formulated according to whether they are linguistic, communicative, or skills-focused.

3 Imagine you are teaching a group using the material shown, *American Think Level 2*. One of the goals of the class is vocabulary development. Write a subsidiary aim that reflects this. How could you achieve the aim?

4 SOCIAL NETWORKING

OBJECTIVES

FUNCTIONS: giving advice
GRAMMAR: indefinite pronouns
(*everyone, no one, someone,* etc.)
all / some / none / any of them;
should(n't), had better, ought to
VOCABULARY: IT terms; language
for giving advice

READING

1 **SPEAKING** Work in pairs. Answer the questions.

1 Which of these social networks do you know about?
2 What do you think of them?
3 Do you know about any other social networks?

2 **SPEAKING** Read these statements about using social networks. Which of them are true for you? Discuss them with a partner.

1 I've got a Facebook account but hardly ever use it.
2 I don't post many comments, but I like to read other people's posts.
3 I constantly check for updates on social media.
4 I sometimes post comments that I regret later.
5 I know of a post that created a problem.

3 ◁ 1.28 Read and listen to the article about online behaviour to decide if each sentence is correct or incorrect. If it's correct, mark it A. If it's incorrect, mark it B.

1 James Miller did not think before he wrote a post and so he lost his job. ☐
2 His boss apologised for giving James work that wasn't very interesting. ☐
3 Cathy's birthday party ended in disaster because her parents went out that evening. ☐
4 A study from last year shows a lot of teens had problems because of their behaviour on the web. ☐
5 The writer of the article thinks that you can't make everybody happy with your posts. ☐
6 He says that before writing a post you should think of reactions you might get. ☐
7 He thinks that we need to be as friendly online as we are in real life. ☐
8 He says that posting things when you're unhappy is a good way to feel better. ☐

4 Work in pairs. Correct the statements marked B.

Think before you act online

Sometimes what we post on our favourite social networks can have consequences we didn't expect. One weekend, 20-year-old James Miller posted on his Facebook page that his job was 'soooo boring'. When he got to work on Monday his boss told him to clear his desk and get out. He gave him a letter, too. It said: 'After reading your comments on Facebook about our company, we understand you are not happy with your work. We think it is better for you to look for something that you will find more interesting.'

A few years ago, a girl's birthday party turned into a nightmare. Fifteen-year-old Cathy posted an invitation to her birthday party online. She posted her address, too. When her parents got back from the cinema that evening, they couldn't believe their eyes. There were 500 people at the party, and some of them were smashing windows, breaking potted plants and making a total mess of the house.

Most teens think they know everything about social media, and that things like this could never happen to them. A study shows that last year alone, more than three million young people worldwide got into trouble because of their online activities.

Here are some important tips. None of them can guarantee 100% Internet security, but all of them will help you to be safer online.

RULE 1: Share with care!

Not everyone will like what you write on Facebook or Twitter. Think before you post something. You can never completely control who sees your profile, your texts, your pictures, or your videos. Before clicking 'post', everyone should ask themselves two questions: 'How will I feel if my family or teachers see this?' and 'How might this post be bad for me in three, five or ten years from now?'

RULE 2: Be polite when you write!

Imagine someone is unfriendly in real life. You don't like it, right? Well, the same is true of online communication. Politeness matters, and anyone can be polite. No one likes it when you 'shout' in your messages. DON'T USE ALL CAPITALS!!!!!!!! If you feel angry or frustrated while you're writing a message, wait a bit. Read it again later and then send it.

RULE 3: Protect and respect!

Don't share your passwords with anyone. Don't post your home or email address online. Beware of 'cyberbullying' – don't forward rumours about other people, and don't say negative things about them. If you get messages like that or see them online, talk to an adult you know.

■ THINK VALUES ■

Responsible online behaviour

1 **Read the statements. Write them in two lists under** *Do* **and** *Don't*.

- say bad things about other people online.
- talk to your teacher or another adult if you get bullied on social media.
- think carefully before you write a post about yourself or other people.
- write a post about someone when you are angry with them.
- write posts containing personal information about your family.
- think before you post a photo of yourself or someone else.

2 SPEAKING **Work in pairs. Compare your lists with your partner. Think of at least two more statements for each list.**

American Think Level 2

Is she your sister?

GRAMMAR
be present:
am, is, are

1 Complete the positive ☺ and negative ☻ sentences with 'm, 're, 's, 'm not, aren't, isn't. 🔊 1.10 Listen to check. ℗

☺
1 Hi, I *'m* Sally.
2 You _____ Krishnan.
3 This is James. He _____ my husband.
4 We _____ Rob's parents.
5 They _____ Rob's friends.
'm = am   's = is   're = are

☻
6 I _____ his sister. I'm his girlfriend.
7 Sally _____ Rob's colleague.
8 Rob and Krishnan _____ brothers.
isn't = is not   aren't = are not

2 Complete the questions ❓ with Are and Is. 🔊 1.11 Listen to check. ℗

❓	✔	✘
1 _____ you Rob's father?	Yes, I am.	No, I'm not.
2 _____ Krishnan your colleague?	Yes, he is.	No, he isn't.
3 _____ they your parents?	Yes, they are.	No, they aren't.

Akio Junko
me — Kenji
Rumi Simona

3 a Write your name and the names of five people you know. Put a line between the people who know each other.

b Work in pairs. Look at your partner's names and write five questions about the people with is and are.

Is Junko your sister? Are you Simona's friend? Are Akio and Rumi colleagues?

Grammar reference and practice, p132

SPEAKING

4 Ask and answer questions.

Is Junko your sister?

No, she isn't. She's my ...

English Unlimited Elementary

KEY WORDS FOR TEACHERS

Check you know the meanings of these terms.

- *main aim*
- *subsidiary aim*
- *linguistic aim*
- *communicative aim*
- *skills-focused aim*

REFLECTION

Look at these questions written by trainee teachers for their trainers after they have been teaching.

a Can you answer any of the trainees' questions?
b If not, what further information would help you to give advice?

Andrzej:

My lesson was meant to be about reading but the learners seemed to be enjoying the lead-in, the speaking activity, so much and they were all using English so I didn't want to stop them. But that meant that I didn't have much time for the reading. Do you think I should have finished the speaking activity sooner?

Sophie:

I started teaching and I thought the atmosphere was awful. The students seemed so bored. They had just already done a long reading lesson before my lesson and there was no energy. I missed out some of the controlled practice of the new language because I just wanted to get to the game, which was more lively. I thought the lesson got better after that. Should I have done all the controlled practice? I know they were still making mistakes at the end.

Samira:

I don't find this elementary class very easy and wasn't very happy with that lesson. I wanted to teach language for talking about plans – but by the time I had explained 'going to' and the present continuous, and gone through how to make the sentences negative and how to make questions, the lesson was just about over and there was no time for any practice.

Jane:

There was a listening exercise in the book with a few comprehension questions. I know this class really loves learning new expressions so I used the transcript to teach things like 'not bad', 'quite nice' and 'pretty good' – ways of expressing evaluation. Do you think I should have just stuck to the book?

Reference

Tsui, A. (2009). Teaching Expertise: Approaches, Perspectives and Characteristics. In A. Burns and J. C. Richards (eds.), *The Cambridge Guide to Second Language Teacher Education*. New York: Cambridge University Press.

27 Lesson planning: lesson design and staging

A Warm-up

1 Choose one of the following sentences and complete it.

A good lesson is like a film, because …
A good lesson is like a football, match because …
A good lesson is like a meal, because …
A good lesson is like a symphony, because …

2 Find somebody who chose the same sentence stem as you. Did you complete the sentence in a similar way?

B A common lesson format: PPP

PPP stands for the broad stages of a popular lesson format – Presentation, Practice, Production.

1 Work in pairs. Put these stages of a lesson in a logical order. How long would you expect to spend on each stage in a 45-minute lesson?

Level: Intermediate
Aim: To focus on the differences in form and use between the past simple and past continuous

Stage	Time	Interaction	Activity
		Ss-Ss	The teacher divides the class into three groups. Each group makes up a story.
		T-Ss Ss-T	The teacher asks questions to check understanding. Learners respond.
1	0–5	T-Ss Ss-T Ss-Ss	The teacher asks learners about their favourite stories when they were young. Learners volunteer stories and/or work in pairs to tell their favourite stories.
		T-Ss Ss-T	The teacher confirms and/or clarifies the form with examples, as necessary, and then gives out a series of rules of use of the verb forms. Learners decide which rules go with which verb form and pick out examples from the text.
		Individual	Learners complete sentences, deciding whether the past simple or continuous is more appropriate.
		Ss-text	The teacher gives out a short story and asks learners to underline examples of the past simple in blue and underline examples of the past continuous in red.
		Ss-Ss	The teacher forms new groups, comprising one person from each of the other groups. The learners tell each other their stories.

2   Compare your solution with that of another pair of trainees. Explain why your order is logical.

3   Identify three stages of the lesson after which the teacher could usefully check that the learners have correct answers.

4   Answer the questions.

Presentation	1 Which stages in B1 constitute the presentation of the new language, including its contextualization?
	2 How is the new language item contextualized?
Practice	3 Which stage in B1 gives 'controlled' practice?
	4 In what sense is this 'controlled'?
Production	5 Which stages in B1 constitute the production stage of the lesson?
	6 What would you expect a teacher to do after the learners have had the chance to use the language?

C A common lesson format: Task-based learning

1   Read this teacher's description of a lesson, based on task-based learning, and then answer the questions below.

> I told the learners about a game I like to play, where you think of who you would invite to your dream dinner party and I told them who I would most like to invite to my dinner party – Nelson Mandela, Frida Kahlo and Charlie Chaplin – and why I would like them to be at my party. The students then planned who they would like to invite, before working in groups to come up with an agreed list of six people for their co-hosted party. I listened while they discussed and helped when they needed vocabulary. Each group then reported back and afterwards we each said whose party we would most like to be at. We then went over some of the language they had used and how they could improve it. As well as correcting some errors, I highlighted some useful words and phrases – things like that.

> [A task is] a piece of classroom work which involves learners in comprehending, manipulating, producing or interacting in the target language while their attention is principally focused on meaning rather than on form.
>
> David Nunan, 1989

a   What was the main task?
b   What happened before the main task?
c   What happened after the main task?

2 a The teacher also said: 'I played the learners a recording of some expert users of English playing the same game.'

Where would you put the recording in the lesson sequence?

b The teacher also said: 'I often get my learners to repeat the task after they have done it once, or to do a very similar task.'

What advantages do you think repeating the task might have?

3 Work in groups. Design a lesson around the task below. Think of pre-task, task and post-task stages. Allocate approximate timings that you would expect to spend on each stage, assuming a 45-minute lesson. Include the interaction patterns that would be likely to occur. Assume that the learners are at B2 level and are studying a general English class.

> Work in small groups. You have £1,000,000 to donate to charities and good causes. Decide together how you will distribute the money.

D Giving advice

Look at the comments made by teachers below. Can you think of any advice that would help them?

1 I have to use a coursebook and it uses a PPP format. There's always a text, the book takes some sentences from the text, we analyse them and practise them. It's ok, but it gets repetitive. I'd like to have more communication at the start of the lesson.

2 We use PPP in my school a lot, but it can be frustrating because we often run short of time and the production phase has to be cut short.

3 My students definitely expect some traditional grammar teaching but I think they need more communication activities, so I am not sure of the best way forward.

4 I like the idea of TBL, but I am not sure it will work. My learners are only elementary level and they need more support before they speak.

5 I have used TBL and the learners enjoyed it, but because I didn't know what new language items I would be teaching I couldn't provide any practice, and I felt bad about that.

KEY WORDS FOR TEACHERS

Check you know the meanings of these terms.

- *task-based learning (TBL)*
- *task*
- *pre-task*
- *language focus*
- *PPP (presentation, practice, production)*

REFLECTION

1 Are there any similarities between PPP and TBL lessons? What are the principal differences?
2 Complete the sentences. Then compare your ideas with a partner.

1 Learners' needs and interests should be considered when ....

....

2 A good lesson usually includes a variety of ....

....

3 There is more than one way that teachers can ....

....

4 Communication phases of lessons can be placed ....

....

5 The language focus of a lesson can be placed ....

....

6 Most lessons should include both communication and ....

....

Reference

Nunan, D. (1989). *Designing Tasks for a Communicative Classroom*. Cambridge: Cambridge University Press.

28 Lesson planning: planning beyond the single lesson

A Warm-up

1 Work in groups. Suggest how these complaints from learners could have been avoided.

Emiliano:

> I used to like the lessons when I started but all we ever do is the coursebook. It's really boring now.

Eriko:

> The teacher does new things with us every day, but I can't remember everything about what we have done before.

Sophie:

> I don't think all the things we do are useful. I wish the teacher would give us more chance to say what we want to do in lessons.

Thomas:

> We have two teachers every morning. Before the break we did a long reading text, and then after the break the next teacher did a reading lesson too. It was so boring.

Suriya:

> I can't prepare for lessons because I never know what the teacher is going to do next. I find the class quite difficult, and it would be better for me to do some work before the lesson.

2 Look at the quote below. What things can a teacher do to create coherence between lessons?

> [Expert teachers] are able to relate their lessons to the entire curriculum and to other curricula and to establish *coherence* between lessons. Novice teachers, by contrast, see individual lessons as discrete units rather than as units in an organized curriculum.
>
> Amy Tsui (2009) [original emphasis]

B Schemes of work

A *scheme of work* (also sometimes called a *timetable*) is a teacher's plan for a sequence of lessons. Depending on the context in which they are working, teachers may be expected to produce a scheme of work for a week, a term, or even the entire year.

1 Work in pairs. Think back to all the lessons for learners of English that you have seen on your course. List the different types of lesson, according to the main focus. For example: the main focus was a grammar presentation.

2 Work with someone from your teaching practice group.

a What different types of lesson has your group taught?
b Has there been a good balance of content?
c Has there been a variety of interaction patterns in lessons? What impact has that had on the energy levels in the room and the pace of the lesson?
d If you have taught at different levels, have you found the classes to be different in terms of the balance of content, interaction patterns and pace?

3 Consider the following teaching contexts. In what ways might a scheme of work differ in each context? Think about:

- the balance of grammar v skills lessons
- the balance of receptive v productive skills
- the inclusion of functional English lessons (often with a focus on language use in social situations), of review lessons, and of practice tests
- the balance between teacher-fronted and learner-centred activities
- the balance between intensive activities and more relaxed activities

A A group of 12 elementary adult learners, studying two evenings a week for nine months in their home country.
B A group of 20 intermediate teenage learners, studying three hours a day for a month in a private language school in Australia.
C A group of 15 upper-intermediate learners preparing in their own country for the IELTS exam, a good result in which will give them access to university study; they have two months of classes, studying 20 hours a week.
D A one-to-one class for an advanced student of business English, that takes place three hours a day for two weeks at their place of work.
E A group of migrant workers and refugees studying in the UK; they have two three-hour lessons a week for thirty weeks. None of the class is above CEFR level A1, and some have additional literacy needs.

C Sequencing lessons

Look at the scheme of work and answer the questions below.

Level: B1 Intermediate
Number of lessons: Three lessons per day, three days per week
Course: General English, including a focus on both language skills and language systems

	Monday	Wednesday	Friday
9–9.50	Grammar – uses of *should* and *must*	Speaking – role play: job interviews	Functional language – asking for advice
10–10.50	Listening – working in a call centre	Speaking and writing – preparing a news story	Speaking – jobs
11–11.50	Grammar revision – present perfect simple	Reading – how to do well in a job interview	Vocabulary – collocations with *make*

1 In terms of quantity in the week, do you think that there is a reasonable balance between vocabulary, grammar and skills work?
2 Is there a reasonable balance of lesson types on each day?
3 Are there obvious links between the lessons that might be better exploited?

D A lesson sequencing puzzle

Work in groups. Use the cards your trainer gives you to plan the lessons for the week. Then compare ideas with another group.

	Monday	Tuesday	Wednesday	Thursday	Friday
9–9.50					
10–10.50					
11–11.50					
12–12.50					

KEY WORDS FOR TEACHERS

Check you know the meanings of these terms.

• *scheme of work* • *recycling* • *needs analysis*

REFLECTION

Work as a group. Look at the coursebook that you are using in Teaching Practice and use it as the basis for planning a sequence of lessons. Your trainer will tell you how many lessons you should plan.

• ensure that there is a variety of types of lesson
• you can use additional material to that provided in your coursebook if you wish

Reference

Tsui, A. (2009). Teaching expertise: Approaches, Perspectives and Characteristics. In A. Burns and J. C. Richards (eds.), *The Cambridge Guide to Second Language Teacher Education*. New York: Cambridge University Press.

29 The online classroom v the face-to-face classroom

A Warm-up

1 Imagine it is two years after your CELTA course. You are now a professional teacher. Close your eyes and picture the lesson you are teaching.

- Where are you, the teacher? What are you doing?
- What is around you while you are teaching?
- Where are the learners? What are they doing?

Draw a picture of what you imagined.

2 Work with a partner. Compare your pictures. What is similar? What is different?

3 If you drew a face-to-face classroom, now imagine an online classroom. If you drew an online classroom, now imagine a face-to-face classroom. What would your answers to activity 1 be now? Tell your partner.

B Different classroom, different activities?

1 With a partner, decide whether the activities below would work best in an online classroom, a face-to-face classroom, or equally well in both. Say why. Check with your trainer if there are any activities which you are not familiar with. One example for each category has been given to help you.

a collaborative writing
b learners write short written responses to a question for everybody to see
c error correction through the use of gestures
d running dictation
e class surveys
f pronunciation drills
g scavenger hunt, e.g. find something old/red/useful
h interviewing guests from outside the class
i board race

Online	switch your camera off, change something around you, switch it on and ask learners to spot the difference(s)
Face-to-face	gallery activities, e.g. reading excerpts from a text around the room
Both	pair and group work

2 Work with another pair to compare your ideas. Can you think of any other ideas not already listed?

C Possible opportunities and challenges

1   Your trainer will divide you into two groups. Group A: think about online classrooms; Group B: think about face-to-face classrooms. Answer the following questions:

i   What are at least three possible advantages for teachers and learners working in this type of classroom? How do learners benefit from these? How can teachers exploit them?
For example: In an online classroom, using breakout rooms allows learners to work together without the background noise of the group. Teachers can exploit breakout rooms by giving different groups secret challenges or personalized tasks to complete, which can then be shared with the whole class.

ii   What are at least three possible challenges for teachers and learners working in this type of classroom? How can you work around these challenges?
For example: It can take longer to work through the same amount of content in an online classroom than a face-to-face classroom. One solution would be to ask learners to prepare for some parts of the lesson before meeting, perhaps by doing a grammar activity or listening to a recording that would otherwise be used in the lesson.

2   Work with somebody from the opposite group. Compare your ideas. Can you suggest other ways to exploit opportunities or work around challenges?

D Adapting a lesson

Think back to a previous TP. Imagine you are teaching it again, but in a different type of classroom. For example, if you taught an online lesson, you are going to teach it in a face-to-face classroom.

With a partner, answer the following questions:
* (If your partner did not observe the TP you are describing) What activities did you include in the lesson? What teaching techniques did you use?
* Can you use the same activities in your alternative classroom? If yes, how would you need to adapt them? If not, what activities could you use to achieve the same aim?
* Can you use the same teaching techniques? Do you need to adapt them for your new classroom? If not, which techniques could you use instead but with a similar outcome?
* What challenges might teachers and learners have with this lesson in the alternative classroom? How can you solve them?
* What opportunities might there be in the new classroom? How can you exploit them?

KEY WORDS FOR TEACHERS

Check you know the meanings of these terms.
* *synchronous (learning/teaching)*
* *asynchronous (learning/teaching)*
* *educational technology (EdTech)*

REFLECTION

Complete at least three of the following sentences:

I will be able to teach in an online classroom, because I already know how to …

To be a better online teacher, it would be useful for me to learn …

I will be able to teach in a face-to-face classroom, because I already know how to …

To be a better face-to-face teacher, it would be useful for me to learn …

One thing I learned today about online/face-to-face teaching is …

One thing I would like to learn more about connected to online/face-to-face teaching is …

I feel … about teaching online/face-to-face classes, because …

30 Choosing and using teaching resources

A Warm-up

Think about materials you have used as a language teacher (for example, the coursebook you are using during the CELTA course) or a language learner (for example, a self-study language learning app). Complete the table with your ideas. Here are some areas you might want to consider:

- engagement and motivation
- language explanations and practice
- skills testing and teaching
- design and ease of use
- sense of progress
- other

	What you liked about the materials	What you didn't like about the materials
As a teacher		
As a student		

Compare your table to a partner. Do you have similar opinions about what you liked and didn't like?

B Criteria for evaluating materials

1 Your trainer will divide you into four groups. Look at the criteria for choosing material below. Add to the possible list of questions.

---

1 Suitability for learners

Are the materials appropriate to the learners' age group?

What do the learners need English for? To what extent do the materials meet these needs?

. . .

---

2 Suitability for teachers

Do the materials require more planning time than the teacher might normally have?

Do the materials support teacher development, for example through teacher's notes?

. . .

---

3 Suitability for the context

Are the materials affordable?

Is there sufficient preparation for any formal assessments learners have to take?

. . .

---

4 Suitability of language and skills focus

Do the materials reflect the version of English (e.g. British English) needed and used by the learners?

Do the reading and listening texts reflect authentic language use?

. . .

---

2 Work in pairs. Select six to eight questions from B1 which are particularly relevant to your current TP group.

C Sources of materials and resources

1 Which of these materials and resources have been used during your CELTA course so far? Which of them would you like to use?

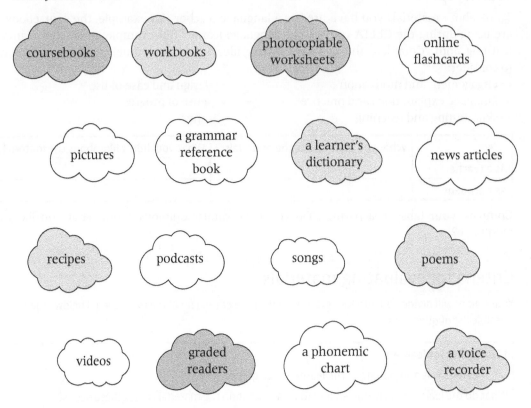

2 What other materials and resources can you add to the list?

3 Work in pairs. Your trainer will give you some materials. Use your shortlist of questions from B2. Decide how likely you are to use the materials with your current TP group.

A conscientious teacher whose teaching is by necessity or choice based on a coursebook will want to do something to compensate for the lack of match between such considerations as teaching context, course aims and learner needs on the one hand and what the coursebook assumes and provides on the other. In short, a coursebook should be seen as a resource for teaching and learning, rather than a body of material to be taught.

Ian McGrath, 2016

D Adapting materials

1 Once you have identified suitable materials for your learners, you need to decide how to use them in your lesson(s). The table shows some of the ways in which you could adapt materials during the lesson planning process or in the lesson itself.

Match the key words (1–4) to the explanations (a–d).

1 Keep	a Switch out one activity or method for another, e.g. a different controlled practice activity.
2 Supplement	b Take out whole stages of an activity or a lesson, e.g. not using a reading text. OR Take out questions from an existing activity.
3 Remove	c Use the materials or activities unchanged.
4 Replace	d Add new materials, e.g. an activity from the teacher's book. OR Add extra questions to an existing activity.

2 Look at as many different examples of materials and resources as you can within the time limit your trainer gives you. Decide:

- whether you would use them with your current TP group
- specific ways you could adapt materials or make use of resources to suit your TP group (including the level of challenge/support provided), your teaching style and your context

Aim to come up with ideas under as many different headings from D1 as possible.

3 Work with another pair. Summarize what you discussed in D2, and decide how useful the questions you selected in B2 were when evaluating the materials.

Check you know the meanings of these terms.

- *authentic materials*
- *engagement*
- *materials evaluation*
- *materials adaptation*
- *differentiation*
- *coursebook, workbook, teacher's book*
- *flashcard*
- *graded reader*
- *learner's dictionary*
- *phonemic chart*
- *realia*

REFLECTION

Choose one of the following questions to answer.

1 How might your choice of questions in B2 have been different if you were considering the following types of learner?
   a young learners
   b university students
   c a company executive who you teach one-to-one
2 Have you enjoyed using a coursebook? How has it helped you? How have you adapted the book for your group? What problems have you found with it?
3 Have you used any materials that were not originally created for teaching (e.g. a song or a video clip)? If so, what were the challenges? What worked well?

Reference

McGrath, I (2016). *Materials Evaluation and Design for Language Teaching* (2nd edition). Edinburgh: Edinburgh University Press.

31 Teaching with limited resources

> It is as well to remember that language is life itself, and that life is very largely language … Language is not a sterile subject to be confined to the classroom. One of two things must be done: either life must be brought to the classroom or the class must be taken to life.
>
> Peter Strevens, 1956

A Warm-up

Imagine you're going to teach in a place where there are no available resources, nor any digital technology. Make a list of six things you might take with you, and put them in the order of importance.

Here are some ideas:

- a grammar of English
- a grammar of the local language
- a bilingual dictionary
- a coursebook
- a picture dictionary of English
- a student grammar of English plus exercises
- the collected short stories of a contemporary writer
- a selection of popular magazines
- a teacher's resource book of language practice games
- your photo album
- a book of jokes for children
- a traditional English songbook
- blank notebooks and pencils

Make your own choice and then, in groups, try to agree on a common list.

B Teaching in difficult circumstances

1 Your trainer will read a short text. As soon as they have finished, try to write down as much as you can remember. Then compare in groups. The trainer will then read it again, and you can make any changes.

2 In the same groups, try to predict what the young teacher did, in the circumstances. Your trainer will then tell you what actually happened.

3 The activity you have just done is a version of what is known as 'dictogloss'. Work in pairs and answer these questions.

1 What were its different stages?
2 How could you adapt it to teach an item of grammar?
3 Could you use it in your own teaching situation?
4 What are its potential strengths?

C Low resource activities

1 Your trainer will demonstrate three activities using few or zero resources. After each one, work in pairs to complete this table.

	1	2	3
Give the activity a name that describes it memorably.			
What language skills did it involve?			
Was there any obvious grammatical or lexical content?			
How would you rate it in terms of: 1 language productivity? 2 learner interaction? 3 learner engagement?			
Could you do this activity: 1 online and face-to-face? 2 with a one-to-one student? 3 with young learners? 4 with a range of levels?			

D Learner-generated material

Learners bring not only material objects to the lesson but also a wealth of experience, knowledge, opinion, preferences, abilities and needs.

1 Work in pairs. Read these descriptions of classroom activities. Which of the above domains – experience, knowledge, opinion, preferences, abilities, needs – does each one tap into?

1 'One of us': Learners work in groups of four, asking each other questions, so as to generate as many true sentences, as possible using this rubric:

One of us	can
Two of us	
Three of us	
All of us	
None of us	

Each group reports to the class.

2 'Five finger exercise': Draw the outline of a hand on the board. Students do the same on a sheet of paper. At the tip of each finger and the thumb write these prompts: a name, a place, a number, a date, and a symbol (e.g. emoji, logo). Instruct students to use the prompts to write something that is significant for them (and that they are prepared to share). Demonstrate by using examples from your own life. In pairs (or mingling), students ask and answer questions about each other's 'hands' (which can then be displayed around the classroom walls). Ask individuals to report on anything interesting they discovered.

3 'Class poll': Establish a topic (it may be the topic of the current coursebook unit, e.g. travel, health, homes). Ask learners to create a survey or questionnaire on the topic in order to find out what the majority thinks about the topic. They first prepare questions in groups, and then are redistributed into new groups to ask and answer their survey questions. They then re-join their original group in order to collate the answers, using a rubric such as 'X out of Y students think that … '. A spokesperson from each group then reports their findings to the class.

2 Work in pairs or small groups. Choose one of the above activities.

1 How could it be adapted so as to address another of the learner domains? For example, what effect would there be if you changed the verb in the 'One of Us' activity?

2 How can the report stage be developed so as to focus on a specific grammar item or function?

KEY WORDS FOR TEACHERS

Check you know the meanings of these terms.

* *resources v resourcefulness*
* *learner-centredness*
* *dictogloss*

REFLECTION

1 Choose one of these resources that were listed in the warm-up activity.

* the collected short stories of a contemporary writer
* a selection of popular magazines
* a teacher's resource book of language practice games
* your photo album
* a book of jokes for children
* a traditional English songbook
* blank notebooks and pencils

In groups, discuss how you might plan an activity or even a whole lesson around this resource, with the aim of generating authentic language use. Report your ideas to the class.

2 Read the quotation by Peter Strevens at the beginning of this unit. How can you 'bring life to the classroom'? How can you 'take the classroom to life'?

Reference

Strevens, P. (1956). *Spoken Language*. London: Longmans, Green & Co., p.69.

32 Using educational technology

A Warm-up

Think of three examples of when different technology tools (e.g. apps, websites, or hardware such as projectors) were used during your CELTA course so far. These examples could be from your own lessons, other trainees' lessons, input sessions or observations of experienced teachers. For each example, answer the following questions:

- What was the tool used for during the activity?
- Who was in control of the tool? The teacher/trainer? Or the learners/trainees?
- Was the activity a one-off or something which could be repeated later, for example at home after the lesson?
- Do you think the use of the tool benefitted the learners'/trainees' learning or distracted them? Why?

Based on your observations, what do you think a teacher needs to remember when using technology tools in their lessons?

B Factors influencing the use of educational technology

There are many different factors you might consider when deciding whether to use a specific tool with your learners. Choose five factors from this list which you think are particularly important.

- **Learning benefits:** for example, supporting recycling of new language, or allowing real-time communication outside the classroom
- **Ease of use:** the amount of time it might take to set up an activity using the tool, and the amount of technology knowledge and/or English knowledge needed to understand how to use it
- **Synchronous or asynchronous:** whether the tool must be used by everyone at the same time, or whether each person can choose to access it at times that suit them
- **Learner autonomy:** whether the tool can only be used with a teacher or independently by learners as well
- **Functionality:** the range of possible functions the tool has
- **Content availability:** the ability to create your own content or adapt existing content and the ease with which you can do this, and/or the range and quality of ready-made content available
- **Target audience:** the demographic that the tool is targeted at, for example children or businesspeople
- **Security:** including privacy settings, for example whether the tool collects data from users
- **Accessibility:** for example, whether the colour scheme or font size can be changed to help learners with visual impairments
- **Compatibility:** how compatible the tool is with different operating systems, for example on mobile phones, computers or tablets
- **Cost:** whether the tool is free, or what the payment model is if paid

Compare your choices with a partner.

C Opinions about technology and education

Here are some statements about educational technology. Rate each one out of 5: 1 = completely disagree, 5 = completely agree.

1.
> The older the learner, the less comfortable they are with using technology during lessons.

2.
> Technology is a part of our everyday lives. It should be part of our lessons.

3.
> I only want to use websites in lessons if they don't require students to create an account or log in.

4.
> As English teachers, it's not our job to teach learners how to evaluate facts on websites.

5.
> Using online games in lessons is just a gimmick. Learners might enjoy them, but they don't really learn anything.

6.
> You should match the choice of tool with the learner's preferences and goals.

Compare your opinions with a partner. Say why you think this.

So what comes first? Technology or learning objectives? The answer is, neither. The learners come first, and this is why one of the best ways of knowing if, and how much, technology should play a part in your class is by finding out from your learners their attitudes to using technology for language learning.

Graham Stanley, 2013

D Putting it into practice

1 With a partner, choose a technology tool (an app, website or piece of hardware) which you think might be beneficial for your learners. Make a list of what a teacher might need to know or consider before using the tool with their learners. Use your priorities in task B and opinions from task C, and any other factors you consider important.

2 Think of three possible activities you could use the tool for in your lessons.

3 Present your tool and activities to another pair. Listen to their presentation. Do you think that their tool and activities would be beneficial to your students? In what way?

KEY WORDS FOR TEACHERS

Check you know the meanings of these terms.

- *educational technology*
- *synchronous learning/teaching*
- *asynchronous learning/teaching*
- *learner autonomy*

REFLECTION

Complete these sentences in as many ways as you can:

When using educational technology, it's important to …

A tool I have used in my teaching is …

A tool I have used in my learning is …

A tool I'd like to experiment with using is … because …

Compare your endings with other trainees.

Reference

Stanley, G. (2013). *Language Learning with Technology*. Cambridge: Cambridge University Press, p.9.

33 Organizing and managing a class

A Warm-up

Your classroom management is the way that you manage students' learning by organising and controlling what happens in your classroom . . .
- Or the way that you consciously decide *not* to organise and control.
- Or the way that you delegate or relinquish such control to the learners.

It is also what happens (or doesn't happen) when you avoid or remain ignorant about these choices.

Jim Scrivener, 2012

1 Work in pairs. What do teachers of any subject do to organize and control (what is happening in) the classroom? List at least five things. For example, give instructions or put learners into pairs or groups. Don't include 'teaching content related to the subject' in your list.

2 Compare your list with another pair. Are any of the ideas on your list only applicable to a face-to-face classroom? Or to an online classroom?

B Organizing learners

1 There are many different ways of organizing learners during lessons, each with advantages and disadvantages.

Your trainer will divide you into two groups. If you are in group A, look at page 180. If you are in group B, look at page 182. Complete the table with your own ideas.

Compare your completed table with somebody from the other group. Was there anything you hadn't thought of?

2 Which of the interaction patterns you discussed in B1 have you observed in lessons or input sessions so far? How many different interaction patterns were used in the session overall? What effect do you think this had on the pace of the lesson/session and learner/trainee engagement in the activities?

C Group dynamics

Read this quote from Sarah Mercer.

Whether we are in online or face-to-face classrooms, our learners need to feel psychologically safe and it is time well spent ensuring that they do. Especially in the language classroom, which depends so heavily on interaction and student engagement, learners must feel secure. When they do, then they will be comfortable to engage in classroom life. They'll be able to use the language without fear of being embarrassed or ridiculed, and feel a sense of belonging in the group.

Sarah Mercer, 2020

Think of at least two ways in which teachers can help learners to feel secure and psychologically safe in the classroom. Compare your ideas with a partner.

D Using the whiteboard

Work in pairs. Say what the pictures below suggest about the best use of the whiteboard, and how this might be the same or different when making a record of information which comes up during an online lesson for learners.

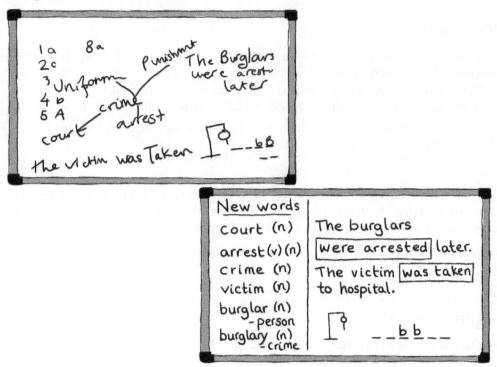

E Grading language

One of the most important things that teachers have to learn is how to adjust their language to make it appropriate for different groups of learners, particularly lower-level learners.

Read sentences a–g. Tick five sentences that offer good advice. Cross out the other two sentences. Then compare your answers with a partner.

a   Pronounce each word slowly and deliberately.

b   Use gestures, pictures and other things that will support what you are saying, to make it easier to understand.

c   Speak with natural rhythm and intonation.

d   Miss out small words (articles, prepositions, auxiliary verbs and so on), so that learners can focus on the 'content' words and understand the message.

e   Speak at a natural speed, but pause slightly longer after each 'chunk', if necessary.

f   Try to avoid 'difficult' vocabulary (for example, very idiomatic language).

g   Try to avoid complex grammar patterns.

F Trainees' queries

As part of the training process, trainees are asked to write an evaluation of their own lessons.

1 Read the trainees' reflective comments, and discuss possible solutions to the problems that they express.

Trainees' comments:

1 I wasn't sure what to do when they were writing sentences. I knew they hadn't all finished, but I didn't want the others to wait too long doing nothing.

2 I didn't enjoy it much. There were a few students who just spoke their own language the whole way through. I did say 'in English' once but it didn't do much good.

3 I wasn't sure what to do in the pair work bit. I thought my instructions were OK, but it was obvious when they started that some of the students hadn't understood, and so I tried to go round to each group and sort it out. I think they did get it in the end, but some of them had finished and others hadn't started.

4 The learners were all doing the pair work exercise in breakout rooms and I just waited in the main room. I was worried they might stop talking if I entered the room. I wasn't sure what I should do, really.

5 I tried to ask more learners questions today. I know I just kept asking the same people in my last lesson. But it was embarrassing. I asked Kim what she thought and she was so quiet I couldn't hear her. Even when I got really close to her it was still difficult.

6 I really wanted to use pair work but I had an odd number, so I did the activity with one of the students. Was this right?

---

2 Now match the trainees' comments (1–6) with the trainer's advice (a–f).

Trainer's advice:

a

Waiting in the main room at the beginning of the activity is OK because it gives the learners some space to make a start. Once they've done this, you should drop into the rooms to hear how things are going and make sure that all learners are on task, but don't interrupt if everything is going well. Just listen to what they say and make some notes. You could also turn off your camera before you enter breakout rooms, to make learners less likely to start speaking to you, rather than continuing to speak to their partners.

b

OK – you did well to sort the problem out, but quite a lot of time was wasted, particularly for the last pair you got to. If there's a fairly general problem, don't be afraid to stop the activity and give the instructions again.

c

Yes, that learner speaks quietly. If you get closer to learners they often get even quieter because they talk to you – not the class. Try getting further away and saying something like 'a bit louder, so everyone can hear'.

d

I thought you made a pretty good decision here. You have to get the right balance. Have something ready for the fast finishers to do, like checking and correcting some of their sentences. You can also set time limits rather than achievement limits, for example 'Write as many sentences as you can in five minutes.', rather than 'Everybody write five sentences.'.

e

> If you do this, it becomes very hard for you to know what the other learners are doing, or to respond if they need help or guidance. You need to think about how you will deal with awkward numbers before the lesson – usually a group of three for pair work is fine and can be managed.

f

> I think part of the problem was that they didn't quite understand what you wanted them to do at times. It was good that you said something but you probably needed to be a little more assertive about it, or consider demonstrating the activity. You could also move learners around a bit so that they are not always sitting next to people who speak the same language.

3   Ask your trainer any other questions you have about classroom management.

KEY WORDS FOR TEACHERS

Check you know the meanings of these terms.

- *classroom management*
- *monitoring*
- *mingling*
- *pace*
- *engagement*
- *grading language*
- *group dynamics*
- *interaction pattern*

REFLECTION

Think about the next lesson that you are going to teach in teaching practice.

- Consider the interaction patterns. Will these be the same throughout the lesson?
- How will you keep a record of new information for students to see during your lesson, such as extra vocabulary or corrections? Will you use a whiteboard or another method? When would it be appropriate to remove what you record?
- At what points in the lesson will you monitor the learners? What will you be looking and listening for?
- What is one other point which has come up during this session which you think it will be particularly useful or important for you to consider during your teaching practice?

References

Mercer, S. (2020). *Nurturing the Relationships in our Classrooms*. Cambridge: Cambridge University Press. https://www.cambridge.org/elt/blog/2020/09/23/nurturing-relationships-in-our-classrooms/

Scrivener, J. (2012). *Classroom Management Techniques*. Cambridge: Cambridge University Press.

34 Managing an activity

A Warm-up

Your trainer will set up two activities.

What was helpful and unhelpful about the way they set up the activities?

B Stages of activity set-up

1 Here is a list of things a teacher might do when setting up and running an activity. Put them in a logical order. (There may be more than one order.)

☐ Demonstrate the activity.
☐ Get learners' attention.
☐ Check learners have understood the instructions.
☐ Give a clear signal for learners to finish.
☐ Follow up on the content of the activity (for example, by checking answers or eliciting ideas from students).
☐ Allow learners to compare their answers or ideas with other learners.
☐ Monitor learners' progress during the activity.
☐ Feedback on the language of the activity (for example, by correcting errors or clarifying the meaning of vocabulary items).
☐ Give the instructions orally while indicating the relevant areas of the material to be used.
☐ Give a clear signal for learners to start.

2 Which of these things did your trainer do when setting up the activity during the warm-up? To what extent did they help you to understand what was expected of you as a learner?

C Strategies for managing an activity

1 The type of activity you are setting up, and the type of learners you are working with, influence how you might set up an activity. Look at the list of classroom management strategies (A–K). Which strategies could be useful if you are setting up:

• an activity where adult students work alone to complete sentences by putting the verb into the correct tense, as specified in the written instructions?
• an activity where university students work in small groups to prepare a presentation?
• an activity where young learners work in open class, guided by the teacher, to draw and write about a monster?
• an activity where teenagers work in pairs to design their perfect school?
A Put learners into pairs or groups before you give them any of the other instructions.
B During your instructions, display materials clearly by holding them in front of you or putting them on the screen, rather than having learners look at materials in front of them.
C Break instructions into small stages. Wait for students to complete one stage before you introduce the next.
D Keep the language of instructions as simple and straightforward as possible. Check that learners have understood them.

155

E Demonstrate how to do the activity.

F Have an example of a finished model prepared, so that you can show learners what they are aiming for.

G Write key words on the board / in the chat box to summarize the instructions, for example *10 minutes, 3 ideas, notes only.*

H Set a time limit so students know how long they have to complete the activity.

I Have a clear purpose in mind for your monitoring. For example, are you checking whether students are on task? Or whether they've finished? Or whether they've got the answers right? Or taking notes of language being used and its accuracy and/or appropriacy? This may change throughout the activity, but can help you to choose what to focus on at each point.

J Ensure learners know all of the answers before you move on to the next activity.

K Follow up on the content of an activity before you correct errors or upgrade language.

You can also add your own ideas.

2 How might your use of these strategies be the same, or different, if you are teaching online or in a physical classroom?

> **Tip**
>
> When planning your lessons, you might want to script instructions and add reminders about anything else you need to do to manage an activity. After the CELTA course, it's unlikely you'll continue to plan in this much depth. However, thinking through activities in detail during the course can help you to anticipate potential problems with activities, feel more confident during lessons, and better support your learners' learning.

D Putting it into practice

1 Choose an activity you are going to use in your next TP. Plan how you will manage the activity.

2 Share your plan with a partner and look at their plan. Check you have both thought about all of the applicable stages of the activity set-up cycle. Can you think of any ways to make the management of the activity more streamlined or straightforward for the teacher or the learners?

KEY WORDS FOR TEACHERS

Check you know the meanings of these terms.

- *classroom management*
- *monitoring*
- *feedback*

REFLECTION

Work in a small group. Choose one aspect of activity management which you think will be most challenging for you, and most beneficial for your learners if you can improve it. Decide with your group how you can work on this, including things you could ask your colleagues to look out for when observing you during TP.

35 Teaching young learners and teenagers

A Warm-up

1 What experience do you have of the following age groups? Tick the relevant boxes.

	2–6 years old	7–12 years old	13–16 years old
I have/had children that age			
I've got family that age (e.g. cousins/siblings)			
I've taught them a lot			
I've taught them a little			
I've worked with them in a non-teaching position a lot			
I've worked with them in a non-teaching position a little			
None			

2 Compare your experiences with these age groups to those of your partners. How do you think you would feel about teaching English to each of these age groups?

B Characteristics of different age groups

Your trainer will allocate you to one of the following age groups:
- Very young learners (2–6 years old)
- Young learners (7–12 years old)
- Teenagers (13–16 years old)

For your age group, answer the following questions with your partners.
- What are the characteristics of this age group? What can they do? What can't they do?
- EITHER What kind of activities work well with them? What don't work?
  OR Find one activity for this age group which you could share with your fellow trainees.
- What can go wrong in the lessons? What can you do to prevent/resolve these issues?

Summarize what you learn in a method of your choice, for example as a poster, a document, or a presentation. Don't forget to include your sources.

Be prepared to tell others about your research.

C Sharing projects

Share what you learned with trainees from a different group. What are two key differences between each age group?

D Project-based lessons

Today's session was an example of a project-based lesson. Answer the following questions with a partner.

1 What are the possible benefits and drawbacks of using project-based lessons?
2 How did your trainer set up and run the session to make the project as successful as possible? Consider aims, support, roles, and sharing projects.
3 What age groups do you think would benefit from project-based lessons?
4 What topics could work well as projects?

KEY WORDS FOR TEACHERS

Check you know the meanings of these terms.

- *very young learners (VYL)*
- *young learners (YL)*
- *project-based lessons*
- *routines*

REFLECTION

1 How might the following areas be different when working with different age groups:

- activity set-up?
- lesson content?
- classroom management?
- lesson types?

What other areas do you think might be different?

2 Think back to the warm-up. Now that you have found out more about working with different age groups, how do you think you would feel about teaching English to each of them?

36 Teaching at different levels

A Warm-up

1 Read these five descriptions of learner proficiency and answer the questions.

  a Which one describes the highest level?
  b Which one describes the lowest level?
  c What order would you put the other three descriptions in (from highest to lowest)?

i	Can understand the main ideas of complex text on both concrete and abstract topics, including technical discussions in their field of specialisation. Can interact with a degree of fluency and spontaneity that makes regular interaction with users of the target language quite possible, without imposing strain on either party. Can produce clear, detailed text on a wide range of subjects and explain a viewpoint on a topical issue, giving the advantages and disadvantages of various options.
ii	Can understand and use familiar everyday expressions and very basic phrases aimed at the satisfaction of needs of a concrete type. Can introduce themselves and others, and can ask and answer questions about personal details such as where someone lives, people they know and things they have. Can interact in a simple way, provided the other person talks slowly and clearly and is prepared to help.
iii	Can understand a wide range of demanding, longer texts, and recognize implicit meaning. Can express themselves fluently and spontaneously without much obvious searching for expressions. Can use language flexibly and effectively for social, academic and professional purposes. Can produce clear, well-structured, detailed text on complex subjects …
iv	Can understand sentences and frequently used expressions related to areas of most immediate relevance […] Can communicate in simple and routine tasks requiring a simple and direct exchange of information on familiar and routine matters. Can describe in simple terms aspects of their background, immediate environment and matters in areas of immediate need.
v	Can understand the main points of clear standard input on familiar matters regularly encountered in work, school, leisure, etc. Can deal with most situations likely to arise whilst travelling in an area where the language is spoken. Can produce simple connected text on topics which are familiar or of personal interest. Can describe experiences and events, dreams, hopes and ambitions and briefly give reasons and explanations for opinions and plans.

Council of Europe *Common European Framework of Reference for Languages*, p.175

2   Read the text about the Common European Framework and label the descriptors in the table above.

> **The Common European Framework**
>
> The *Common European Framework of Reference for Languages* (CEFR) 'presents a comprehensive descriptive scheme of language proficiency' (page 27). It provides descriptors of learners at three broad levels: A: *basic user;* B: *independent user;* and C: *proficient user.* Each level is divided into two bands: A1, A2; B1, B2; C1, C2. The descriptors in the table represent levels C1, B2, B1, A2 and A1.

Common European Framework of Reference for Languages Council of Europe

3   Think about the TP group you are currently teaching. What level are they? Do you think these descriptors reflect their abilities?

4   Complete these sentences in any way that seems appropriate to you. You can use ideas from the CEFR descriptors or your own ideas.

   a   At higher levels, learners might need …
   b   At lower levels, learners might need …
   c   The learners in my current TP group are … level, which means that in our lessons …

   Compare your ideas with a partner.

B   Adapting to different levels

1   Look at these comments made by two CELTA trainees. Maria moved from teaching an elementary class (i.e. CEFR A1–A2) to teaching an upper-intermediate class (i.e. CEFR B2). Salim moved from teaching the B2 upper-intermediate class to teaching the A1–A2 elementary class. Which person do you think made each comment?

a
In the other group, I didn't mind if the learners used their own language a bit – but I try to keep it to an absolute minimum now.

b
I realize that the learners I have now can already say a lot of what they want to, and my job is partly to give them alternative ways of saying things.

c
I got a real shock when I started with this new group. I don't think they understood anything I said in the first lesson! There was an activity that was quite easy but I just couldn't get across what they had to do.

d
I sometimes found it difficult to explain how to use our online platform. I had to remember to carefully show them what to click on and where to type, not just tell them.

e
I've noticed that I have more activities in a lesson and they tend to be a bit shorter – particularly, pair and group work doesn't last as long.

f
I really have to work hard to research grammar now. The learners sometimes ask quite difficult questions and my research helps me to feel more confident.

g
I can't just chat to this group and find out about them as people so easily. I don't think I have such a good rapport with them.

2 Work in pairs. Compare your experiences.

    a Have you had any similar experiences to Maria and Salim with your current TP group?

    b Is there anything else which has surprised or interested you about the level(s) you have taught so far?

C Productive skills

1 Work in pairs. Read this speaking activity from an elementary coursebook and answer the questions.

    a How do the materials support the learners before they speak?

    b Can you predict the sort of exchanges that would happen in activity 5c?

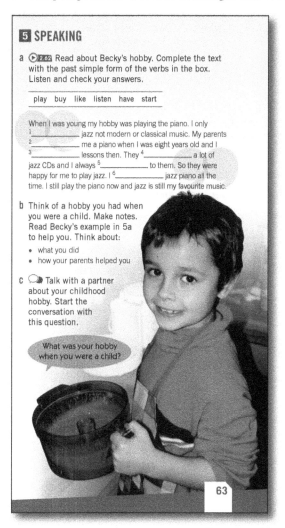

5 SPEAKING

a ▶ 2.62 Read about Becky's hobby. Complete the text with the past simple form of the verbs in the box. Listen and check your answers.

play buy like listen have start

When I was young my hobby was playing the piano. I only ¹_____ jazz not modern or classical music. My parents ²_____ me a piano when I was eight years old and I ³_____ lessons then. They ⁴_____ a lot of jazz CDs and I always ⁵_____ to them. So they were happy for me to play jazz. I ⁶_____ jazz piano all the time. I still play the piano now and jazz is still my favourite music.

b Think of a hobby you had when you were a child. Make notes. Read Becky's example in 5a to help you. Think about:
- what you did
- how your parents helped you

c 💬 Talk with a partner about your childhood hobby. Start the conversation with this question.

What was your hobby when you were a child?

63

Empower A2

2 a Work in groups. Discuss how you would expect a higher-level speaking activity to be the same or different.

b Now look at the following activity from an upper-intermediate coursebook.
Are the activities the same or different in the ways you predicted?

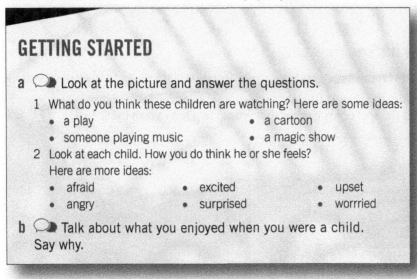

GETTING STARTED

a 💬 Look at the picture and answer the questions.

1 What do you think these children are watching? Here are some ideas:
- a play
- someone playing music
- a cartoon
- a magic show

2 Look at each child. How you do think he or she feels?
Here are more ideas:
- afraid
- angry
- excited
- surprised
- upset
- worrried

b 💬 Talk about what you enjoyed when you were a child. Say why.

Empower B2

3 How would you expect writing tasks to differ between lower and higher levels?

D Receptive skills

1 Read the following listening transcript. What level do you think it would be appropriate for: elementary, intermediate, or advanced? Why?

CD3 31

CAROL The most important moment in my life was um the day I met Owen. An old friend was having a party, but the weather was so bad that I nearly didn't bother going. Just think, if I'd stayed at home, I wouldn't have met my husband. Anyway, my friend introduced me to Owen and we got on really well. He was only in London for a few days – he's American, you see – and he was supposed to fly back to Boston the following day. But the next morning Owen called me to say that Heathrow airport was closed because of ice and snow. He'd have flown home that day if the weather hadn't been so bad. Anyway, he invited me out for lunch and we got to know each other a bit better. He flew home the next day, but by that time we were already madly in love. We got married two years later – and the rest, as they say, is history.

face2face

2 Read how three teachers used this listening text at different levels. Match the lesson descriptions with the levels: elementary, intermediate and advanced. Think about what features of the activities helped you to decide on the level.

---

a 'I told the learners that they're at a party and they overhear Carol. The next day they meet a friend and they want to retell Carol's story. They listened once, then worked with their partner to retell the story. After that, they listened again to see what details they had forgotten. They discussed what aspects of Carol's storytelling style had made certain parts of the story more memorable than others.'

---

b 'I displayed pictures of the different events in the story, for example a party, a man and a woman meeting, a snowy airport, and a wedding. The learners predicted the order of the events, then listened and checked if they were correct. I played the recording two or three times, letting them discuss the task in pairs between each playing. I then handed out the transcript for them to listen one final time.'

---

c 'I dictated the following questions:

1 Where did Carol meet her husband?

2 Where is her husband from?

3 Why couldn't he fly home?

4 When did they get married?

Then I played the recording, checked the answers and re-played the bits they were having trouble with. I played the recording another couple of times and asked the learners to pick out phrases that helped Carol to tell her story. Finally, the learners talked in pairs about memorable moments in their lives.

---

3 Work in groups. Discuss what these tasks suggest about dealing with listening texts at different levels.

⬛ Teaching grammar

1 Work in groups. Discuss how you would expect grammar input to differ between levels.

Consider:
- the type of context used to present the language
- how much is taught
- the complexity of the rules that are given
- the type of practice activities that are used

2 Work in groups. Discuss the aspects of grammar input that you would expect to remain the same at different levels.

3 Compare the two coursebook extracts on the next page. One is taken from a beginner coursebook and the other is taken from an upper-intermediate course book.
- In what ways are the extracts similar?
- In what ways are the extracts different?
- How well do they match what you discussed in activities E1 and E2?

3 GRAMMAR: Statements with *be going to*

A **Circle the correct answer. Use the sentences in the grammar box to help you.**
  1 Use *be going to* to talk about **things you're doing right now / future plans**.
  2 Make future statements with *be going to* + **a verb / a noun**.

> **Statements with** *be going to*
>
> | | |
> |---|---|
> | I**'m going to be** home tomorrow. | I**'m not going to be** home tonight. |
> | It**'s going to be** light all night. | It **isn't going to be** light all night. |
> | You**'re going to meet** me at the airport. | My friends **aren't going to go** shopping. |
> | We**'re going to get together** with some of my friends. | They**'re not going to eat** outside this weekend. |

B **Complete the sentences with *be going to* and the affirmative or negative form of the verb in parentheses ( ).**
  1 I _____ (be) home tomorrow. I have to work at the office.
  2 My parents _____ (take) me to lunch on Saturday. They're busy.
  3 My friends and I _____ (go) on a trip to Rio next year. We have our tickets!
  4 I _____ (study) a lot next week. I have an important test.
  5 My friend _____ (meet) me tonight. She's sick.

C PAIR WORK **Change the sentences in exercise 3B so they're true for you. Then compare with a partner.**
> I'm not going to be home tomorrow. I have to go to college.

D ▶ Now go to page 137. Look at the grammar chart and do the grammar exercise for 10.1.

Evolve 1

---

3 GRAMMAR: Future forms

A **Read the sentences in the grammar box. Circle the correct options to complete the rules.**

> **Future forms**
>
> It **won't cause** you stress but **will give** you a real sense of satisfaction.
> Eventually I**'m going to edit** it.
> I**'m not showing** it to them until it's done.
> In a couple of years, I**'ll be looking for** a job.
> This video **is going to be** a useful example of my skills as a filmmaker.
> If things go smoothly, I **might start** my own video production business one day.

  1 Use *be going to*, *will*, or ***don't / won't*** for predictions, expectations, or guesses about the future.
  2 Use *be going to* or the **present continuous / simple present** for future plans and intentions.
  3 Use *will* + *be* + verb + *-ing* for **an action in progress / a finished action** at a time in the future.
  4 Use *might*, *may*, or *could* when you're **certain / uncertain** about the future.

B ▶ Now go to page 136. Look at the grammar chart and do the grammar exercise for 8.2.

C **Write six sentences on plans and predictions about your work, studies, or side projects. Use a different future form from exercise 3A in each sentence. Check your accuracy. Then compare with a partner. Are any of your predictions similar?**

 ACCURACY CHECK

Use the future continuous, not the present continuous, for an action in progress in the future.

In a couple of years, I'm looking for a job. ✗
In a couple of years, I'll be looking for a job. ✓

Evolve 5

Check you know the meanings of these terms.

* *CEFR*
* *beginner, elementary, intermediate, advanced, proficiency*
* *grading language*

REFLECTION

Think about the level you have just been working with on your course. Work with the rest of your teaching practice group and complete the chart below with information which might be useful for your colleagues when they take over the class. Then compare your charts with a partner from another teaching practice group.

Advice for teaching my class

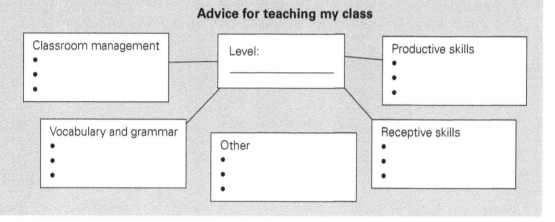

Reference

Council of Europe (2020), *Common European Framework of Reference for Languages: Learning, Teaching, Assessment – Companion volume,* Council of Europe Publishing, Strasbourg, available at www.coe.int/lang-cefr. p.175

37 Maintaining learner motivation

A Warm-up

Think about the following questions for a few moments and then discuss them with your partners.

1 What was the reason for you choosing to do the CELTA course? What is your goal?
2 What things have helped keep you motivated during the course?
3 Have any things demotivated you during the course?
4 Think about the learners you have been teaching. What are some of the reasons that they are learning English?
5 What things do you think have impacted on their motivation, both since they started learning and also since the start of this particular course?
6 Are there any similarities between your experiences and those of your learners?

B Supporting motivation

Look at the quote below.

> A common experience for many learners and teachers is that motivation, however strong to begin with, will ebb and flow through the learning process, subject to many internal and external influences over a course of study or even within the space of a single lesson.
>
> Ema Ushioda, 2012

What things might cause motivation to 'ebb and flow', both over a period of time and in a single lesson?

2 Work in pairs to complete the text by reading it to each other. Trainee A should complete the version of the text on page 181. Trainee B should complete the version on page 183. Trainee A should start.

3 Look back at the completed text and answer the questions.

a Can you give some examples of teacher behaviours that would indicate that they are motivated?
b How might a teacher build interest in a reading activity before learners see the text?
c How could teachers give some control to learners over their learning, including lesson content and delivery style?
d How might a teacher help learners to feel a sense of progress and mastery of the language?

C Learning from learners

1 Look at following situations and complete the sentences.

A 'My English is OK for most things, I think. I really want to improve though, but don't really know what to work on.'
The teacher should help the learner to set ...
B 'I love it when my teacher lets us choose what to do. Last night she gave us three different bits of homework and we did the one we wanted.'
This is one way to give learners ...

C 'The teachers are really good. They make sure everyone is polite and friendly in the class. When I make mistakes, I know people won't laugh at me. The best thing about the class is meeting up with everyone.'
This shows how important it is to …

D 'I used to really enjoy English last year. It was good fun and the teacher was always smiling. The first few minutes of the class was always talking about what show we were streaming, or something like that. But the new teacher doesn't smile at us and never asks about our interests.'
It is important that a teacher …

E 'I need English mainly for travel – booking hotels, going to restaurants and things. The class is OK, but it can be a bit boring. It is mainly about grammar and so I don't really feel ready to use English for the things I need.'
Ideally the teacher needs to make the classes more …

2 Work in small groups. Consider the learners you have been teaching as part of your course. What things do you think motivate them? Are there any things that demotivate them? Try to be as specific as you can.

D Putting it into practice

1 Work in small groups. Look at the following short piece of material. How could you make it more interesting?

1 **Look at Jane and Maria. What things can they do?**

Jane: swim ✓	juggle ✓	speak three languages ✗	sail a boat ✓	sing ✗
Maria: swim ✗	juggle ✓	speak three languages ✗	sail a boat ✗	sing ✓

Example: *Jane can swim but Maria can't.*
Write more sentences about Jane and Maria.

2 **Ask and answer. Look at the information about Jane and Maria. Work with a partner. Ask and answer questions about them.**

Can Jane swim?

Yes, she can.

3 **Now you. Write three sentences about what you can do.**

2 Explain how you adapted the material to another group.

KEY WORDS FOR TEACHERS

Check you know the meanings of these terms.

- *motivation*
- *goals*
- *relevance*
- *(learner) autonomy*
- *mastery*
- *personalization*

REFLECTION

1 Write five 'golden rules' for motivating language learners that you will aim to implement in your teaching. They may refer to either the teaching you are currently doing as part of your CELTA course or your teaching after the course.

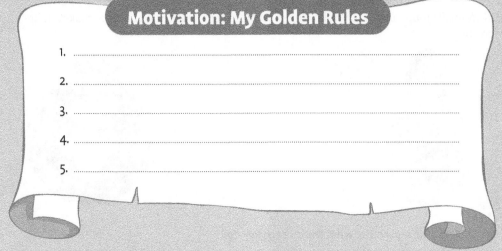

Motivation: My Golden Rules

1. ....
2. ....
3. ....
4. ....
5. ....

2. When you are ready, compare your list to a partner.
3. Which of your rules do you think are easiest to implement on an ongoing basis? Do you envisage any being difficult to implement?
4. Set a reminder on your phone to review these principles when you start teaching.

Reference

Ushioda, E. (2012). Motivation. In A. Burns and J.C. Richards (eds.), *The Cambridge Guide to Pedagogy and Practice in Second Language Teaching*. New York: Cambridge University Press.

38 Introduction to assessment

A Warm-up

1 Answer as many questions as you can in five minutes.

> **Revision Quiz**
>
> 1 How is the future continuous formed?
> 2 Which form is best, and why?
>   i Ah, let me look at my calendar – yes, here's Laura's appointment, *I'm meeting/I'll meet* her on the 14th.
>   ii People *will work/are working* entirely from home in a few years.
>   iii Who do you think *will win/are winning* the football match tomorrow?
> 3 What things does a learner need to know about new vocabulary items?
> 4 In what ways is a physical class different to an online class?
> 5 How can a teacher help to keep learners motivated?

2 If this test had been designed to measure your progress on the CELTA course, to what extent do you think that it would be fair? How could it be improved?

> ... testing is not, of course, the only way in which information about people's language ability can be gathered. It is just one form of assessment, and other methods will often be more appropriate.
>
> Arthur Hughes, 2003

B Some key terms

Use the words below to complete each sentence.

assessment	formative	practical	reliable
test	valid	washback	

1 _____ refers to the collection of information about a learner's language ability and progress. It can be carried out in many ways, including formal and informal situations, and scoring may be objective or subjective.
2 A _____ is one form of assessment. It may be formal or informal, and has connotations of objectivity and being completed individually.
3 An assessment is considered _____ if it measures what it is supposed to measure. This often involves ensuring that the content of the assessment is appropriate.
4 An assessment is considered _____ if the results are consistent. Two learners of the same ability should receive the same outcome in the assessment.
5 An assessment is _____ if it can be carried out within the constraints of the situation. For example, it has to be done within the specified timeframe and within any financial constraints.
6 _____ is the effect that the assessment method has on teaching. It may have a positive impact (making teaching more effective) or a negative impact.
7 _____ assessment is assessment that is carried out during a course with the goal of improving learning. For example, teachers might take the data into account when planning future lessons.

C Reasons for assessing learners

1 Work in small groups. Look at the following assessment situations, and in each case think why the assessment may be taking place.

   a A course director is expecting an intake of 100 students. They will all sit a test on the first morning of the course.

   b A teacher has a new class. In the second lesson they decide to give the class a short piece of assessment.

   c A teacher has taught 50 hours of a 100-hour course. They decide to give the class a formal piece of assessment.

   d A class is very near the end of their course. In the penultimate lesson, they will have a test.

2 Work in small groups. Can you think of any other reasons why teachers may want to test learners? Can you think of any disadvantages to testing learners?

D Ways of assessing learners

1 There are many ways of gathering information about a learner's abilities. Look at the methods listed below and answer the questions that follow.

	Examples
Observation	*A teacher monitors classroom activities carefully, forming an impression of which learners are progressing most quickly.*
Portfolios	*Learners keep a record of their homework tasks, along with the feedback they receive. They also reflect on their performance in specific classroom activities. The portfolios are reviewed by the teacher periodically.*
Self-assessment	*The teacher provides learners with a list of things that have been covered in recent lessons. Learners mark each item with one of the following to indicate their level of understanding:* ☺ ☺ ☹
Multiple choice questions	*I'm _____ to see Zoe tomorrow.* *a) gone b) go c) going d) went*
Gap-fill exercises	*'What is your _____ film?' 'Casablanca – it's great.'*
Sentence transformations	*The shop sold the last copy of the book yesterday.* *The last copy of the book ....*
Writing a composition	*You see the following job advert in a newspaper. Write a letter of application.*
Oral interviews	*Learners are shown pictures and describe what they can see.*
Sentence production	*Learners write sentences about themselves using a given structure, such as used to + infinitive.*

   a Which of these assess individual language items?
   b Which of these assess language items in combination?
   c Which can be marked objectively?
   d Which require subjective marking criteria?

2 Choose one of the following areas:
- receptive skills
- productive skills
- vocabulary and grammar

Decide which of the assessment types in 1, above, could be used to assess your chosen area.

3 What features make one learner's spoken language better than another's? For example, a learner may use a wider range of vocabulary than another.

Imagine that you want to give an oral test to a group of learners. Work in a small group and design some criteria by which you can assess performance.

E How not to assess

Look at the following complaints from learners. What was the problem with the assessment design in each case? Complete the sentences.

1 'The instructions just said 'fill the gaps' – so I did and got nearly all of the questions wrong because I was only supposed to use one word. A lot of the students did the same as me.'
Instructions need …

2 'The course was all about listening and speaking and I really liked it – but then we had to do a writing test and I didn't do very well.'
The content of the test should …

3 'It was a writing assessment and we had to write a reply to a letter. I didn't do very well because I didn't understand the letter, so I put the wrong information in the reply.'
Input data (the information the test taker responds to) needs to be …

4 'I got the test back from the teacher and I hadn't done very well. I was the worst in the class. The teacher just wrote 'You must work harder' at the bottom, but I was working quite hard.'
Feedback should …

5 'It was obvious that the teachers marking the essays had completely different ideas on what should get a good mark. It was really unfair.'
Markers of assessments should …

F Teaching exam classes

Exams are a type of assessment which have some formal, public significance. They are generally linked to a specified level of what a successful candidate can accomplish in a language. There are many different ELT exams and teachers often teach classes that are geared towards preparing learners for a particular exam.

Agree ●————————————————————————————● Disagree

For each of the numbered statements below, decide where you would place it on the cline.

1 It is a good idea to start with a past paper of the test, so that learners know what they are working towards.
2 Learners in exam classes are usually more goal-oriented than those in a general English class.
3 The most important thing is to ensure that learners understand the requirements of the exam.
4 The teacher should make teaching exam strategies the main focus of each class.
5 The learners in an exam class will always be highly motivated.
6 The most important thing in an exam class is that learners become familiar with exam-style questions.
7 In preparation for the exam, it is a good idea to give learners the marking criteria for subjectively marked parts of the exam (such as speaking) and ask them to grade themselves.
8 Teachers of exam classes need to know exactly what the exam consists of and how it will be graded.

KEY WORDS FOR TEACHERS

Check you know the meanings of these terms.

* *assessment*
* *test*
* *validity*
* *reliability*
* *practicality*
* *washback*

REFLECTION

1 Answer the questions below.
   a In your experience, what impact do regular assessments and tests have on learning?
   b How can a teacher ensure that feedback on assessment is constructive?
   c What are the advantages of including self-assessment in a course?
   d How can a teacher avoid negative washback effects when teaching?

2 Think about what your own teaching practice students have learned since you've been teaching them. Design a short assessment that would be appropriate for them.

Reference

Hughes, A. (2003). *Testing for Language Teachers* (2nd edition). Cambridge: Cambridge University Press, p. 173.

39 Developing as a teacher

A Warm-up

1 Think of something which you have become very good at. It could be learning a language, a musical instrument, a sport, a hobby (such as cooking), or anything else. How did you first learn? How did you continue learning? Tell your partner.

2 Work with a partner. Talk about what you consider to be the most useful parts of the CELTA course. However, you can only say one word at a time. Do not plan what you will say beforehand. You must listen to each other so that sentences are coherent and grammatically accurate.

Example:

Trainee 1	I		the		practice		etc.
Trainee 2		enjoyed		teaching		because	

3 Could you use an activity type such as 2 in your teaching? If so, how?

B Professional development

1 Indicate with a cross how much impact the following parts of the CELTA course have had on your learning. Compare your ideas with a partner.

Input sessions	big impact ——————— not much impact
Planning teaching practice lessons	big impact ——————— not much impact
Teaching	big impact ——————— not much impact
Post-teaching feedback discussions	big impact ——————— not much impact
Writing evaluations of your own lessons	big impact ——————— not much impact
Researching and writing course assignments	big impact ——————— not much impact
Websites for teachers and online forums	big impact ——————— not much impact
Tutorials with tutors	big impact ——————— not much impact
Course reading, e.g. handouts, articles, chapters from books	big impact ——————— not much impact
Observation of peers	big impact ——————— not much impact
Observation of practising teachers	big impact ——————— not much impact
Informal discussions with colleagues	big impact ——————— not much impact
Other (what, exactly?)	big impact ——————— not much impact

2 Work in groups. In the light of the above, discuss ways to continue developing as a teacher after the course.

C Learning from experience

The learning experience that underpins the CELTA course is, essentially, one of 'reflecting on experience'. That is, learning takes place through cycles of action and reflection.

1 Study the reflective learning cycle. Identify some concrete experiences that you have had during the course (e.g. 'a student told me that they really liked the speaking activity in the lesson I did on pets last week'). How did you review that experience? What did you decide to do as a consequence? (How) did it change your teaching? Tell your partner about your experiences.

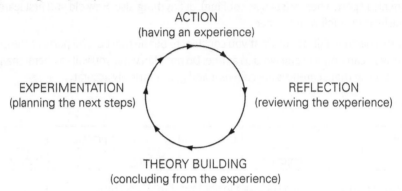

ACTION
(having an experience)

EXPERIMENTATION
(planning the next steps)

REFLECTION
(reviewing the experience)

THEORY BUILDING
(concluding from the experience)

2 Read the quote below.

> Reflective practice occurs . . . when teachers consciously take on the role of reflective practitioner and subject their own beliefs about teaching and learning to critical analysis, take full responsibility for their actions in the classroom, and continue to improve their teaching practice.
>
> Thomas Farrell, 2018

This suggests that teachers can modify both their beliefs about learning and teaching and their practice over time. Work in small groups and discuss the questions below.

a Why do you think this change happens?
b How you can reflect on lessons and continue to improve your teaching practice after the course?
c Can you think of reasons why teachers might not change their practices?

3 Complete the table below, using the terms your trainer dictates.

I will definitely try to do this	I would like to do this but it is unlikely	I don't like this idea much	I don't understand how this helps me as a teacher

D Case studies

1 Read about these teachers. How are the teachers similar and how are they different in terms of their development? Who do you think you will be most similar to?

George	Cara
When I finished my CELTA course, I couldn't wait to start teaching. I was determined that I would try the new things I had learned. If I hear a colleague say they have done something that students liked, I rush to try it out too. Some things work and so I use them again and again. Some things are disasters and I never repeat them! And sometimes I can think of a way of improving it so that it will work. My goal is to start a website where I can share my teaching ideas and also invite other teachers to share theirs. I am already quite active on discussion forums and social media – I just loving talking about teaching!	When I finished my CELTA course, I knew I still had a lot to learn. I was really nervous in the classroom and didn't feel I knew enough. I've always liked reading and I started reading more about teaching: all sorts of things – blogposts but also some journal things. It actually gave me confidence. I remember an experienced teacher talking about something in the staffroom and I knew about it – I had been reading about it – and started to feel I belonged. Colleagues even started asking me questions! I want to go on now and do more courses and get even better qualified. There's so much to learn, and one day I would like to teach other teachers.
Ayala	**Jane**
When I got my first job after CELTA, I was quite nervous going into a new school. The Director of Studies said she wanted to watch me teach and I was so worried, but actually she gave me really good feedback. There were things to work on but it was really helpful and encouraging. There were some development workshops at the school which staff took turns to lead, and they were great. I learned a lot because they were teaching the same sorts of classes as me. After about a year I actually led one of those sessions and the feedback on that was good. I was so proud. I felt I was really contributing to the school.	I did my CELTA course nearly two years ago. I learned a lot on my course but even more when I started teaching. I tried to make friends in the staffroom and found people were really helpful to me and were usually happy to share their experiences. I think I am ready for a new challenge, and I am currently deciding whether to do an MA in TESOL or a Cambridge DELTA course. I know they are both high level and will be hard work. I would really love to end up working in a university so that might influence my choice, but I know a lot of teachers who feel they have benefited from the Diploma because it is really practical.

2 Jane says, 'I am currently deciding whether to do an MA in TESOL or a Cambridge DELTA course. I know they are both high level and will be hard work.'

What information would you like to know about these courses? You could consider such things as:

- entry requirements
- duration
- recognition/value
- modes of study
- assessment
- prices

Ask your trainer any questions you have.

Check you know the meanings of these terms.

- *reflection*
- *observation*
- *teacher beliefs*

REFLECTION

Draw up a 'continue learning' action plan for your first six months of teaching after this course. Make your plan as specific as possible. Then work in pairs or groups and compare your plans.

Reference

Farrell, T. (2018). Reflective Practice for Language Teachers. In J. Liontas (ed.) *The TESOL Encyclopedia of English Language Teaching*. New York: Wiley and Sons.

40 Preparing for the workplace

A Warm-up

Put a tick next to the three things that you think will influence you most in looking for a teaching job.

- working in an organization with a good reputation
- working in an organization with a good professional development programme
- being part of a supportive staffroom within an organization
- gaining as much experience as possible
- earning a decent salary
- staying near family and friends
- travelling
- being in a culture you are already familiar with
- learning about a new culture and a new language

When you are ready, see if you can find anybody who has chosen the same three things as you.

B Finding a job

Your trainer will tell you about some useful websites you could use to look for teaching positions after your CELTA course. Look at two different sites. Find a position you would be interested in applying for.

Work in pairs. Discuss which positions you have chosen and why.

C Job interviews

1   Imagine you are going to apply for the job which you or your partner selected in B. Make a list of questions you might be asked during the interview. Here are some possible categories of questions:

- professional development, including qualifications
- experience
- language awareness
- soft skills, such as teamwork or time management
- strengths and areas to develop

2   Work together to create a list of questions you could ask during the interview. Here are some possible topics:

- learners
- teachers
- syllabus, materials and resources
- pay and conditions
- professional development
- safeguarding
- (if applicable) relocating to another country

3   Compare your lists from C1 and C2 with another pair. Do they have any questions you could add to your list?

4   Your trainer will tell you if you are an interviewer or an applicant.

Interviewers

Use questions from C1 to conduct a short interview. Find out whether the applicant is suitable for the job you chose in B.

After the interview, think about what particularly impressed you in the applicant's answers, and decide on one tip you could give them to improve their interview skills.

Applicants

Answer the questions the interviewer asks.

After the interview, think about which questions were easier or more challenging to answer. What might you need to bear in mind when preparing for real job interviews?

Switch roles and conduct another interview.

D Maintaining health and wellbeing

Read the quote.

> Teacher burnout and attrition rates are at record highs across the globe. Teaching has become a profession frequently characterized by high levels of stress and low professional wellbeing. Yet, research has shown that teachers who experience high levels of wellbeing teach more effectively and more creatively with fewer discipline issues, leading ultimately to higher levels of learner achievement. Quite simply, teacher wellbeing is desirable for teachers themselves as well as for their learners.
>
> Sarah Mercer, 2020

Work in groups. Answer the following questions.

1   What might contribute to high levels of stress for teachers?

2   How do you think high levels of wellbeing might help teachers to 'teach more effectively and more creatively with fewer discipline issues'? How do you think this might lead to 'higher levels of learner achievement'?

3   What could teachers do to help them maintain a high level of wellbeing? Some areas to consider might include: maintaining physical health, time management, professional and personal relationships, and leisure activities.

KEY WORDS FOR TEACHERS

Check you know the meanings of these terms.

- *continuous professional development (CPD)*
- *soft skills*
- *burnout*
- *wellbeing*

REFLECTION

1 Work in pairs. Play 'tennis'. Your trainer will demonstrate how to do this.

   Round 1: What questions might you be asked in a job interview?

   Round 2: What questions could you ask in a job interview?

   Round 3: How can teachers maintain a high level of wellbeing?

2 Think of three tips you could give to somebody who is preparing to work in ELT. Compare your tips to a partner's.

References

Mercer, S. (2020). The Wellbeing of Language Teachers in the Private Sector: An Ecological Perspective. *Language Teaching Research*.

https://doi.org/10.1177/1362168820973510

Pair and group work

Unit 25
Trainee A
Mutual dictation – Integrating skills

You get a text message, you read it .... You read an interesting news story .... You go to a lecture ...., you might pass it on. ...., ..., language skills are not always used in isolation. ...., Think back to the last lesson you taught. ....?

Unit 33
Group A

Interaction pattern	Example activity	One advantage of this interaction pattern	One disadvantage of this interaction pattern
Individual work	Reading comprehension	Learners have some time to concentrate on learning at their own pace.	Learners may be unsure of their answers and therefore not want to share them.
Pair work	Answering discussion questions	Maximizes opportunities for speaking.	
Small group work	Creating a product to 'sell' to classmates		Some learners may be reluctant to participate in small groups, leaving others to do the work.
Two big teams	A whiteboard race	Working as a team can motivate learners to push their English production to higher levels.	
Mingle*	A survey of classmates' opinions		This can be challenging to set up in an online classroom, depending on the platform used.
Teacher leads the class	Drilling pronunciation of a new grammar item	All learners are working on the same thing at the same time, which can (sometimes) be easier for the teacher to control.	
Learner(s) lead(s) the class	Checking answers to a gap-fill activity		Some learners may think that only the teacher should lead the class, and therefore not listen to their classmates.

* In a mingle, learners speak to one or two other learners at a time, moving to speak to the next person when they are ready. They will speak to multiple other learners during the course of the activity.

Unit 34
Trainee A
Present continuous statements

Say what is happening in Picture A. Then find seven differences between Picture A and Picture B.

Picture A

Evolve 1

Unit 37
Trainee A
Motivation

There are many factors which can affect a learner's motivation. One of the most important factors is actually ....
.... , they are more likely to have motivated students. ....
.... they feel that their lessons are useful and relevant to them, ...
.... and tailor lessons to meet those needs. ....
.... intrinsically interesting, and this means that teachers ....
.... before doing them. .... and lesson styles ....
.... Motivation is further boosted when ....
.... over what and how they learn. Finally, another important contributor to motivation is a sense of success and mastery, so teachers need to help learners see the progress that they are making.

Unit 25

Trainee B

Mutual dictation – Integrating skills

You get a text message, ... and you text back. .... and you tell someone about it. .... and you take notes. If you hear some gossip, ... So, outside the classroom, ..., They tend to be combined. .... Were any skills combined?

Unit 33

Group B

Interaction pattern	Example activity	One advantage of this interaction pattern	One disadvantage of this interaction pattern
Individual work	Reading comprehension	Learners have some time to concentrate on learning at their own pace.	Learners may be unsure of their answers and therefore not want to share them.
Pair work	Answering discussion questions		Face-to-face classrooms can get very noisy, and it can be a challenge for the teacher to hear individuals.
Small group work	Creating a product to 'sell' to classmates	Learners can bounce ideas off each other and experiment with their English with supportive classmates.	
Two big teams	A whiteboard race		If there is an element of competition, learners (and teachers!) sometimes forget the English-related goals of the activity.
Mingle*	A survey of classmates' opinions	Learners can speak to lots of different classmates, getting to know everybody better.	
Teacher leads the class	Drilling pronunciation of a new grammar item		Depending on how the teacher runs the activity, learners may disengage and lose interest in the lesson.
Learner(s) lead(s) the class	Checking answers to a gap-fill activity	Learners enjoy being given responsibility, and this can help them to feel engaged.	

* In a mingle, learners speak to one or two other learners at a time, moving to speak to the next person when they are ready. They will speak to multiple other learners during the course of the activity.

Unit 34
Trainee B
Present continuous statements

Say what is happening in Picture A. Then find seven differences between Picture A and Picture B.

Picture B

Evolve 1

Unit 37
Trainee B
Motivation

There are many factors which can affect a learner's motivation. ....
.... teacher motivation. Research suggests that if a teacher is enthusiastic and motivated, ...
.... Learners are also more likely to be motivated if ....
...., so clearly teachers have to understand the
needs of their learners .... Materials and activities also need
to be ...., ... are well advised to build interest
in activities .... Using a variety of activities .... can also make classes
more interesting. .... learners have a sense of control ....
.... Finally, another important contributor to motivation is a sense of success and
mastery, so teachers need to help learners see the progress that they are making.

Teaching practice

Introduction

Teaching practice (often called TP) is a core component of the course and the one that gives the course its essentially practical nature. By giving you the opportunity to teach classes of real learners, TP prepares you for the reality of the classroom, and provides a means for putting into practice the techniques and procedures that are discussed in the input sessions. TP provides an ongoing cycle of planning, teaching and reflection, and thereby provides an experientially-driven model for your future professional development.

TP is timetabled continuously throughout the course. Each centre will organize TP differently, but it will always involve each trainee teaching at least two different groups at a minimum of two different levels. Lessons may vary in length, but in all centres the total of supervised teaching will add up to six hours for each candidate. Each member of your TP group will take it in turns to teach (parts of) the lessons. You will observe while your TP group colleagues teach. After the lesson, the trainer will conduct a feedback session, normally involving other trainees. Part of your assessment is based on your ability to contribute to peer feedback, and to respond in a professional way to feedback which has been given to you.

Check with your trainer how TP is organized at your centre.

To get the maximum benefit from TP, and to ease some of the anxieties associated with it, you may find the following advice helpful.

Planning

Go easy!

You will usually be given a section of a coursebook, or a specific language item (often called a 'TP point') to teach. Stick to this – don't try and teach everything you know about English! If you're asked to teach six items of vocabulary, don't attempt more than six. If you're asked to teach one specific use of a grammar structure, don't attempt to teach all its other uses as well. If you're asked to teach one page of a unit of a coursebook, don't teach the whole unit.

Liaise

It's generally the case that you will be sharing the lesson with your colleagues, each taking their turn in the overall sequence. This usually means that you will be working from the same material. It is imperative, therefore, that you are each clear as to which sections of the material you are working with, so that there is no obvious doubling up. You will also need to check which parts of the lesson sequence are dependent on what has gone before. For example, is the person who follows on from you depending on your having taught some key vocabulary?

Research

Do some research into the language area you are going to teach. See unit 5 for some ideas on how to do this. At the same time, don't simply regurgitate the contents of the grammar reference in your lesson plan. Your job is to make the teaching point accessible and memorable for the learners.

Manage your time

Try not to spend longer planning the lesson than would be reasonable in real working conditions. In other words, don't stay up all night planning a twenty-minute lesson. If you are having trouble coming up with an idea for the lesson, put it aside and do something different – like going for a walk, or cooking a meal. Some of our best ideas come to us when we're busy doing something physical or routine.

Be economical

Don't try and reinvent the wheel. If you have been asked to teach some coursebook material, you don't have to rewrite it or redesign it. Remember that it is your *teaching* skills that are being developed, not your ability as a materials writer or graphic artist.

Be prepared

Allow for the unexpected, e.g. a late start, or a new learner, or a problem you hadn't foreseen. Predict possible problems and consider how you might solve them ready for the lesson.

Be flexible

Keep your plan flexible. Don't try and put more than is realistically achievable into your lesson. At the same time, it's also a good idea to have one extra activity 'up your sleeve', just in case you have time to spare. There are some ideas in the '5-minute activities' section on pages 207–211.

Structure your lesson

Plan around a basic lesson format that makes sense to you and that will make sense to the learners, such as one that has a beginning, a middle and an end. For example, the beginning might be a short ice-breaker, the middle might be the presentation of a grammar structure, and the end might be personalized practice.

Prioritize

Decide what the main activity of the lesson should be: reading, or speaking, for example, or writing, or listening. This will often be specified in the TP point. Make sure your plan foregrounds this core activity, and that it is not pushed to the end of the lesson by lots of preparatory stages.

Build in variety

At the planning stage, think how you will vary the focus throughout the lesson – so that some of the focus is on you, some is on the learners, and some is on a reading text or listening passage, for example. Even in a twenty- or thirty-minute lesson it's possible to have three different activities, and three different types of interaction. If you are not the primary focus of the whole lesson, it is likely to be more engaging for the learners, and will give you more space to pay attention to their needs.

Be resourceful

Don't overburden yourself with materials, such as different documents or websites, unless absolutely necessary. The more 'stuff' you bring into the lesson, the more chance you will lose your way, or things will go wrong. Also, the more you attempt to 'plug every hole' in the lesson, the fewer opportunities there will be for spontaneity and learner participation.

Check with your trainer how lesson planning works at your centre, including the specific documents you need to complete before your lessons.

Teaching

Be ready to teach

Make sure you have everything that you need ready for the lesson. If you have prepared a worksheet, make sure you have sufficient copies. If you are using audio or video, make sure they are set up so you only have to click play. Remember that it doesn't create a good impression if you have to leave the room for something you have forgotten, or if you have to find a document on the computer before you can open it.

Learn their names

Learn and use the learners' names. Check the pronunciation if you are unsure. This is a common courtesy; it also makes classroom management a lot easier.

Don't overrun

You only have a limited amount of time to teach your lesson, and you are likely to be sharing the same class with your colleagues, so it is imperative that you start and finish on time. If you are worried that you may run over time, organize with a colleague, or your trainer, some means by which they signal that you have, say, only five minutes left.

Start on time

The class starts when there are learners in front of you – even if only just one. However, don't launch into your prepared lesson when the bulk of the class still haven't arrived. Spend this time getting to know your learners better, or reviewing the last lesson, or checking homework. Useful questions include: *How was your day? Did you have good weekend? What do you like doing in your spare time?* You can also ask the learner(s) to ask you the same or similar questions. If there are two learners, they can ask and answer these questions in a pair.

Focus on the learners

Focus your attention on the learners throughout your lesson, and not on your trainer or your colleagues. Witty asides to your colleagues are likely to be misinterpreted by the learners and so are generally best avoided.

Look calm

You are likely to feel nervous, but you don't need to *look* nervous. Face-to-face, try and find a 'still point' in the classroom and stay there: it may be seated, or standing. Online, experiment with switching off your self-view, so that you don't focus on what you look like. Try and maintain a natural speaking voice, as if you were not really in a lesson at all. Exploit opportunities for friendly laughter – this helps defuse the tension.

Don't panic!

If you lose your way in the lesson, and are not sure what to do next, don't panic. Stop and consult your plan: there is no requirement to have memorized what is on it. The learners know that you are there to improve your teaching skills, so they are forgiving when there are problems.

Adapt

Even if you think you are running out of time, don't rush. It may be better to skip a stage, if it means getting to your main activity. Be prepared to abandon or adapt parts of your planned lesson if you feel that these parts are simply not working as planned. Remember that during the feedback on the lesson you will have a chance to reflect on your 'in-flight' decisions.

Observe

When you are not teaching, but observing the lessons of your colleagues, give them your full attention. This is not just a question of courtesy: you will learn a lot from watching your colleagues in action, and will be able (and expected!) to discuss their lessons during the feedback session. Also, you can learn a lot about the learners by observing the way they respond to different techniques and teaching styles. However, avoid becoming involved in the lesson in any way – for example, by answering questions that learners may try to address to you. Indicate to the learners that they should ask the teacher who is currently teaching them.

Check with your trainer how TP is conducted at your centre.

Here are some comments on TP lessons. They have been collected from trainers' assessments.

Choose one or two of the problem areas below. Consider how you could avoid them.

- You directed your attention at one half of the class only.
- You added 'OK?' to virtually everything you said.
- You wrote everything on the board in capital letters.
- You allowed one or two learners to dominate.
- You were talking to the learners while you were writing on the board with your back to them.
- After each new word that you presented, you asked 'Do you understand?'.
- You didn't give time for learners to answer your questions. You often answered the questions yourself.
- The learners weren't always clear when they were supposed to pay attention to what you were saying. You kept a sort of running commentary on what you were doing, or going to do, throughout the lesson.
- You started giving the instructions for the activity before you had got the learners' full attention.
- Everything that the learners said you wrote in the chat box, in a rather random way.
- During the pair work stage, you spent a lot of time helping one learner, without noticing that the other learners had finished.
- You adopted a rather unnatural delivery, as if you were speaking to a child, or someone hard of hearing.
- You set up the group work task nicely, but you didn't go round the breakout rooms to check that the learners were doing it properly.
- While the learners were reading the text, you kept distracting them by talking.

Read the positive comments. What can you do to make sure that you receive similar comments during your course?

- You were very calm, and you were able to draw the learners' attention.
- You used a natural but intelligible speaking style.
- You knew all of the learners' names, and made sure they all had a chance to participate.
- It was good that you gave the instructions for the task before putting the learners into their groups.

- Demonstrating the task with one of the learners before they went into pairs seemed to help the learners feel more confident when starting the activity.
- When you realized that the learners were confused, you stopped the task and gave them clear instructions.
- You encouraged the learners to expand on their contributions, from single words and phrases to fuller utterances.
- You responded naturally to what the learners said, before moving on to correct the way that they were saying it in a supportive way.
- The board work was legible and well organized.
- Your use of the camera, microphone, slides and other materials was effective, especially your decision to turn off your camera or microphone or stop screen sharing at times.
- I liked the way you provided individual help to learners when they needed it, while remaining aware of the rest of the class.
- You gave clear, constructive feedback on all of the activities.

Post-teaching

Balance your reflection – don't forget the positives!

Few, if any, lessons go as planned. Be kind to yourself if you feel that yours didn't. Even if you weren't satisfied with the lesson, remember that it is part of the learning process of improving your teaching. Ensure you identify the strengths of the lesson, not only its weaknesses.

Take responsibility

Consider your role in the parts of the lesson which worked well, not just what the learners did. When thinking about the weaknesses, consider what action points you can take away to improve your future lessons. Don't abdicate responsibility for the lesson by, for example, blaming the learners, or the coursebook, or the TP point. Effective teachers adapt to the constraints that are imposed on them.

Reflect

After the lesson, spend some time to reflect on the lesson. On pages 189–191 there are some ways of framing the reflection process, in the form of reflection tasks. Your trainer may assign one of these tasks as the basis for completing your self-evaluation or for the post-lesson feedback session. You may also want to use them to continue to reflect on your lessons after the CELTA course has finished.

Keep a journal

You may wish to keep a training journal – that is, a private written log of your experience learning to become a teacher. You can use any of the reflection tasks to structure your journal. There are some special journal tasks on pages 191–192.

Reflection tasks

Reflection task 1: Questions

Think about your lesson and answer the questions.

- What happened according to plan? Why?
- What *didn't* happen according to plan? Why?
- What happened that I didn't expect? Why? What effect did this have?
- What would I do differently next time? Why?

Reflection task 2: Sentence starters (aims)

Complete the sentences.

- My main aim in this lesson was …
- I achieved my main aim partially/completely. As evidence I would mention …

OR:
- I didn't achieve my main aim because …
- My subsidiary aim(s) was/were …
- I achieved my subsidiary aim(s) partially/completely. As evidence I would mention …

OR:
- I didn't achieve my subsidiary aim(s) because …
- In my next lesson, I'll continue/stop/change/…

Reflection task 3: Sentence starters (impressions)

Complete these sentences in as many ways as you can.

- I was happy with the way … because …
- I wasn't so happy with the way … because …
- The learners seemed to be engaged when …
- The learners didn't seem engaged when …
- Next time, I'll continue/stop/change/…

Reflection task 4: Statements

Complete the table (0 = totally disagree; 5 = totally agree).

Statement	Evaluation	Evidence
1. I achieved what I was aiming to do.	0 1 2 3 4 5	
2. I managed the class effectively.	0 1 2 3 4 5	
3. I involved all the learners.	0 1 2 3 4 5	
4. I used the time effectively.	0 1 2 3 4 5	
5. I used the materials/aids effectively.	0 1 2 3 4 5	
Based on what happened in this lesson, next time I'll continue/stop/change/…		

Reflection task 5: Personal objectives

Before the lesson, write down two or three personal objectives you hope to achieve.

After the lesson, evaluate the extent to which you achieved them.

Write some more objectives for your next lesson.

Reflection task 6: What I learned, and what I still don't know

What did you learn from this lesson? Summarize what you learned in the form of statements.
- I learned that ...
- I learned that ...
- I learned that ...

What are you still unsure about? Summarize your uncertainties in the form of questions. For example:
- Why ... ?
- When ... ?
- How ... ?
- How much ... ?
- ...

Reflection task 7: My report

Write a report on your lesson. Complete the table.

Subject*	Grade (A–D)	Comments
Planning		
Classroom management		
Manner and rapport		
Use of lesson materials		
Use of technology / other resources, e.g. the whiteboard		
Use of learners' L1		
Dealing with pre-planned language		
Dealing with learner language		
Dealing with individuals		
Achievement of aims		
Summary		

* You can add extra 'subjects' if you wish, or put N/A where appropriate.

Reflection task 8: Learner feedback

Work in groups. Design a short feedback questionnaire for the learners to complete in the last few minutes of each lesson. The object of the questionnaire is to give you feedback on the effectiveness of the lessons – but it is *not* to compare teachers. Typical questions might be:
- What was the most important or most interesting thing you learned in this lesson?
- What activity would you like to do again?

- What activity would you *not* like to do again?
- Was there anything missing in the lesson?

Alternatively, provide sentence stems for the learners to complete.

- I learned …
- I enjoyed it when …
- I didn't like it so much when …
- I would like to do more …
- I don't really want to do more …

Collect the feedback forms from the learners at the end of the lesson and compare their responses with your own evaluation of the lesson.

Journal Tasks

Journal task 1: Narrative

Write a narrative account of the lesson, saying what happened.

- Compare this to your plan.
- Explain any departures from the plan.
- Draw some conclusions from this experience.

Journal task 2: Key event

Focus on a 'key event' in the lesson, that is, a significant moment that stands out in your recall of the lesson.

- Why was this event significant?
- What did you learn from it?

Journal task 3: Focus on a learner

Choose one learner to focus on, and keep a journal record of his or her progress over a number of lessons. Record your own assessment and those of your colleagues.

You should do this task with the consent of the learner concerned. You can then ask the learner to read your account and to make their own comments. This will allow you to judge, for example, to what extent your inferences were correct.

Journal task 4: Recording the lesson

With the permission of the learners, audio- or video record a segment of your lesson.

Play it back, and transcribe a section of it.

Analyse this section with a view to answering questions such as:
- How natural is my classroom language?
- How intelligible am I? How clear are my instructions?
- Do I have any obtrusive mannerisms (either vocal or gestural)?
- How naturally do I interact with the learners?

Journal task 5: Feedback and reflection

Record your reflections on the feedback that you were given – by your trainer, by your colleagues, or by the learners themselves.

- How useful was the feedback?
- Was it fair? Was it balanced?
- Did the feedback match your own assessment of the lesson?
- How do you think you will take the feedback into account in planning and teaching future lessons?
- What have you learned about *giving* feedback?

Journal Task 6: Self-evaluation

At periodic points in your journal, such as at the end of each week if you are on a full-time course, answer these questions:

- How am I developing as a language teacher?
- What are my strengths? What are my limitations at present?
- How can I improve my teaching?
- How am I helping my learners?
- What satisfaction does language teaching give me?

Adapted from Richards, J. C and Ho, B.

Reference

Richards, J. C., and Ho, B. (1998). Reflective Thinking Through Journal Writing. In Richards, J. C., *Beyond Training*. Cambridge: Cambridge University Press, p.170.

Classroom observation

These *Observation tasks* are for use when observing the teaching practice lessons of your colleagues, or any other classes that you are required to observe during the course. Each task has a particular focus, and links to some aspect of the course input. Some tasks focus on the teacher, others focus on the learners, and some focus on the interaction between both teacher and learners. These tasks are designed to provide a focus for post-observation discussion. Normally, your trainer will tell you which task you should use.

Note that there is no obligation to compete all the tasks during the course. You may find them useful after the course, if you have the opportunity to observe other teachers.

Below are some commonly observed points of observation etiquette when observing an experienced teacher. Many of these points will also be relevant when observing peers in TP.

- arrive on time
- be polite and courteous at all times
- in a physical classroom, take a seat where the teacher asks you to
- in an online classroom, keep your camera and microphone off unless the teacher asks you to put them on
- keep an unobtrusive presence throughout, and do not participate unless invited to by the teacher
- focus all of your attention on the lesson – do not, for example, be distracted by messages on your phone
- if you have to leave before the end of the class, forewarn the teacher before the lesson starts
- pay attention – if you are taking notes, do this discreetly
- after the lesson, do not make any evaluative comments about the lesson to the teacher
- thank the teacher for letting you observe

Observation task 1

Focus: The teacher's position and body language

Note the teacher's/teachers' position and movement. If possible, draw a ground plan showing the teacher's movements during the lesson.

- When and where do they sit?
- When and where do they stand?
- How near do they approach the learners at different parts of the lesson?
- When do they move around?
- Do they project to all the learners?
- Can they be heard and seen clearly by all the learners?
- Do they use gesture effectively?
- Do they make eye contact with individual learners?
- What impact did the teacher's position and body language have on the learners during the lesson?

Observation task 2

Focus: The individual learners

Make sure you know the learners' names! Observe the learners and complete the table with their names. You can write the name of more than one learner in each box, and put the name of one learner in more than one box.

Names	Behaviour
	take the initiative, volunteer answers to questions, and ask questions of their own
	avoid answering questions, or only answer if called on by name; don't participate much in open class
	take part actively in pair and group work
	tend to take a back-seat role in group work, and do only the minimum in pair work
	take risks with the language, and are not afraid of making mistakes
	are hesitant, even reluctant, to speak
	catch on quickly and follow explanations relatively easily
	often get confused and frequently seek clarification from peers
	[add anything else that strikes you as worthy of comment]

Observation task 3

Focus: Interaction

Observe the different *interactions* in each lesson and complete the table. Then answer the questions.

Teacher – whole class	%
Learners in pairs	%
Learners in groups	%
Learners working individually	%
Other	%

- What is the predominant type of interaction?
- Does it seem appropriate to the aims of the lesson?
- In which interaction were the learners most productive (in the sense of producing most English)?

Observation task 4

Focus: Meaning

Are there any points during the lessons where the learners seem unclear as to what something *means*? How can you tell?

- How is the problem resolved? Does the teacher deliberately seek to *check understanding*?
- How is this done?
- How effective is it?
- What impact did this communication breakdown, and the way it was resolved, seem to have on the learner?

Observation task 5

Focus: Instructions

Are there any points in the lesson when learners seem unsure of what the teacher wants them to do? Why is this, do you think?

Write down, word for word, some examples of instructions that occur during the lesson(s). Are they clear, economical and effective?

Does the teacher do anything else to support their instructions? If so, what?

Observation task 6

Focus: Engagement/Interest

To what extent do the learners seem *engaged* by the lesson? What is the level of learner *interest*? Plot their engagement over the course of the lesson using this graph (100% = maximally engaged; 0% = totally uninterested). Make a note of what was happening in the lesson during any particular peaks or troughs.

Note: You could do this task to record your impression of the group as a whole or of an individual learner.

Observation task 7

Focus: Learner participation

Choose *one* learner to focus on (preferably one that you can see and/or hear well) and answer the questions.

- How much speaking (in English) do they do during the lesson?
- Do they speak in their own language? If so, for what purpose?
- How many contributions do they make in whole-class stages (as opposed to pair or group work)?
- Do these contributions take the form of one- or two-word utterances, or are they longer turns?
- Do you think the learner wanted to contribute more during the lesson? If so, what prevented them?
- Do you think the learner should have contributed more during the lesson? If so, what prevented them?

Observation task 8

Focus: Own language use

Make a note of all the instances in which either a learner or the teacher uses a language other than English.

- At what stage(s) of the lesson does this occur?
- What is the purpose of the communication? (e.g. is it to clarify understanding, ask for help etc.?)
- How effective was it in achieving this purpose?

Observation task 9

Focus: Teacher–learner interaction

Draw a 'map' of the class, and label each learner. For example:

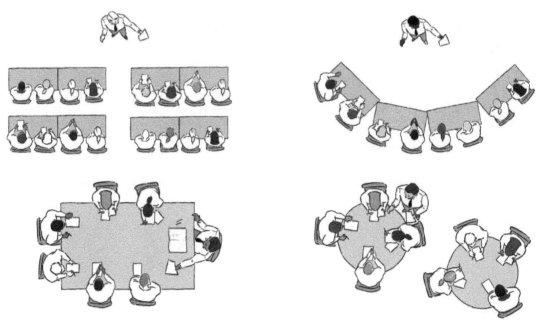

Draw lines and arrows to indicate the different interactions between the teacher and individuals, or between individuals and the teacher. The direction of the arrow should indicate whether the interaction is teacher-initiated or learner-initiated.

For an online class, you might want to draw the layout of the screen, and note who has cameras / microphones on if you think that is relevant.

- What does your interaction map suggest?
- What is the dominant direction of interaction?
- With which learners did the teacher interact with most?
- Which learners initiated most?
- Can you think of possible explanations for your findings?

Observation task 10

Focus: Error and correction

Note down in the table any instances of learner error, the teacher's response (if any) and the learner's response, e.g. self-correction:

Error	Teacher's response	Learner's response

Observation task 11

Focus: Planning and staging

Observe a lesson without knowing in advance how it was planned. As you observe the lesson, note the main stages.

- Is there a clear division into stages? For example, is there a beginning, middle and end?
- How is each new stage signalled?
- What is the aim of each stage?
- If possible, after the lesson compare your impression of the lesson's design with the teacher's plan.

Observation task 12a

Focus: Boardwork (physical classroom)

Note down at what points in the lesson the teacher uses the board.

- Are there clearly differentiated boardwork stages, or is the board used intermittently throughout the lesson?
- What is written on to the board? And where? How legible is it?
- Do the learners copy what is written on the board?
- If possible, ask to look at a learner's book at the end of the lesson, and see if the learner's record of the lesson is an accurate summary of the lesson. To what extent is the learner's record of the lesson a reflection of the boardwork?

Observation task 12b

Focus: 'Boardwork' (online)

For an online lesson, there may not be a clear 'board'. Follow the steps above in 12a and consider anything the teacher uses to share live notes with the learners during the lesson, for example the chat box, online whiteboards, or the use of documents or slides. Focus on notes which are based on what has come up during the lesson, rather than materials which seem to have been prepared before the lesson.

Observation task 13

Focus: Time on task

Draw a pie chart to show the proportion of time on task.

- How much time is spent leading up to tasks (including pre-teaching, giving instructions, etc)?
- How much time do the learners spend engaged on the tasks?
- How much time is spent on the post-task phase (e.g. checking, reporting back, etc)?

Observation task 14

Focus: Roles of the teacher

Complete the table.

Observation sheet		
Does the teacher . . .	**Time/Stage of lesson**	**What happened? Was it effective?**
give instructions?		
check instructions?		
correct errors?		
explain new language?		
monitor pairs/groups?		
say/do anything designed to build rapport?		
The teacher's questions		
What questions does the teacher ask?	What is the function, or purpose, of each question?	

Observation task 15

Focus: Teacher questions

Monitor the teacher's questioning techniques, and answer the questions.

- How many real questions does the teacher ask? (These are questions for which the teacher doesn't know the answer, such as *What did you do at the weekend?*)
- How many display questions does the teacher ask? (These are questions for which the teacher already knows the answer and prompt learners to display knowledge, such as *What is the past of the verb 'go'?*)
- Is there a difference in atmosphere and/or learner behaviour between stages that are dominated by real questions and those dominated by display questions?

Observation task 16

Focus: Teachers' 'in-flight' decisions

Observe a lesson for which there is a detailed lesson plan. Keep a record of how closely the lesson follows the plan, and answer the questions.

- Are there any points where the actual lesson departs from the plan?
- Does the actual timing differ from the planned timing?
- Can you account for these differences?
- If possible, talk to the teacher after the lesson. How does your account of the teacher's 'in-flight' decisions compare to their own?

Observation task 17

Focus: Pronunciation

Is there any focus on pronunciation included in the lesson? If yes, when and for what purpose?

- Keep a note of any pronunciation errors that occur in the lesson.
- Does the error affect communication?
- Is the error corrected? If so, how and by whom?

Observation task 18

Focus: Coursebook use

Observe a lesson that is based on coursebook material. Monitor how closely the lesson follows the coursebook. Use the following cline to record the extent to which the lesson follows the coursebook. (100% = the lesson follows the coursebook exactly; 0% = the lesson bears no resemblance to the coursebook material).

0% _____ 100%

If possible, compare your evaluation with the teacher's own assessment of how closely the lesson followed the coursebook. What was the effect of either following the coursebook closely, or not following it closely?

Observation task 19

Focus: Differentiation

Observe the lesson and make note of any instances in which the teacher adapts a task or the material to make it easier, or more challenging, for an individual, or several individuals, in the class.

- How does the teacher adapt the material?
- What is the impact of the adaptation?

Observation task 20

Focus: Use of technology

Observe a lesson in which the teacher is using some form of technology.

- What technology is used?
- How 'fluent' is the teacher with the use of this technology? Does it contribute to the flow of the lesson, or does it disrupt it?
- To what extent does the technology enhance the lesson?
- Could the lesson aims have been achieved as effectively without it?

Observation task 21

Focus: Teacher talking time

Make a pie chart to show how much time the teacher talks, and how much time the learners talk.

- Who spends more time talking, the teacher or the learners?
- At what points in the lesson do the learners talk more?
- At what points in the lesson does the teacher talk more?
- Approximately how much of the learner talking time is spent talking in open class?
- Approximately how much of the learner talking time is spent talking in pairs and groups?
- Does the teacher ever address individuals or small groups 'privately' (i.e. without the whole class hearing)?

Observation task 22

Focus: You choose!

Decide what aspect of your class you would like your colleagues to observe. For example:

While watching my lesson, I would like you to monitor / observe / note down any instance of the following:
1.
2.
3.

Guide to tutorials

During your course you will have the opportunity to speak to your tutor on a one-to-one basis. Your tutor will keep a written record of your tutorial, which you will need to sign. You will have the opportunity to discuss how you feel about the course generally, and specifically you will talk about your progress with the written assignments and your teaching practice. The tutorials will be based around the 'progress records' in your CELTA 5, which is the document which is filled in to confirm that you have completed all of the course components.

The number of tutorials you have is not fixed, but remember that your tutors will be happy to discuss your progress with you, so you can ask to make additional appointments if you feel you need to. At a minimum, you will have a compulsory tutorial halfway through the course, called a Stage 2 tutorial. The information in this guide refers to this tutorial only, though some of it is applicable to other tutorials you may have.

Before your tutorial

Look at the list of criteria in the CELTA 5. If you do not understand any of them, then look in the back of the CELTA 5, where they are explained. If you are still unsure, ask your tutor to explain them.

For each criterion, you should consider whether you feel you are meeting the necessary standard for this stage of the course. Try to think of examples from your teaching and think back also to the feedback you have received. Remember that you are in the process of learning to be a better teacher, and it is not expected that you are perfect at all the things described in the criteria – in fact, that would mean you are on the wrong course! Remember that being able to evaluate your teaching objectively is a key part of developing as a reflective teacher both during and after the course, which is why there is a focus on it during your lesson self-evaluations and as part of your Stage 2 tutorial.

During your tutorial

Remember, your tutorials are two-way processes – you need to speak and also listen to your tutor. Try to be as honest and open as you can be. If there is anything that you do not understand or that you are having trouble with, do not be afraid to say so.

Your tutorial will be based around the list of points in your CELTA 5. Your tutor will have considered all of the points as part of their evaluation of your progress, although they may not comment on all of them in detail, as time may be limited.

If you need to, make a note of any important points that you wish to raise before the tutorial and take it in with you, so that you do not forget what you want to say.

After your tutorial

Think carefully about what was said. Read the notes that your tutor made and, if you agree with the summary, sign the page in the CELTA 5.

Ensure you understand the points you need to work on, and also how to make progress in these areas. If you are not sure, you could look back at notes you have made during input sessions, read relevant books or blog posts on the topic, watch teacher training videos for CELTA trainees, or ask your tutor for further guidance. When you next teach, try to include evidence of having worked on relevant points in the way you plan the lesson, the way you teach it, and also when you reflect on the lesson in feedback.

Guide to written assignments

There are four written assignments on the CELTA course. They are:
- Focus on the learner
- Language related tasks (including language analysis)
- Language skills related task
- Lessons from the classroom

In total you should write around 3000–4000 words: your centre will give you guidance on how much to write for each assignment. The centre will also give you the criteria by which your work will be assessed. It is very important that you read and understand these before you start writing. The precise requirements of the assignments will vary from centre to centre, but the marking criteria are standardized and are the same in all centres. For each assignment you should read the instructions very carefully, so that you know exactly what you are expected to write. If you are not sure, then ask for further clarification.

The work you submit must be your own. When you include quotes or take ideas from other sources, you must acknowledge where these come from.

If your first submission of an assignment is not up to the required standard, you are allowed to resubmit it one more time. If necessary, you can resubmit all four assignments, once each, without any effect on your final CELTA grade. In order to pass the written component of the course, and therefore the course overall, you must pass three out of the four assignments.

A proportion of all the assignments will be 'double-marked' – that is to say, two tutors will read the assignment and agree on marks. This is a way of standardizing the process and ensuring that it is fair.

Things to remember

Writing can be viewed as a process – there are stages you go through before ending up with the final 'product'. You may find it helpful to clearly distinguish the stages in your mind – research, planning, producing a draft, editing the work, redrafting, checking for spelling and grammar mistakes and so on.

Think of who you are writing for. Your tutor will read the work, but so too may an external assessor. It is important that the tone is not too informal – it should either be in a slightly academic style, or be neutral.

Using headings and sub-headings can help the reader to follow your arguments and are appropriate in most assignments.

All assignments require you to use terminology accurately, so double-check you know what terms mean during the course and ask your tutor if you're not sure.

Things that can go wrong

Time management

Your centre will tell you when you should hand work in. The deadlines are spread throughout the course to help both you and your tutors with time management. It is important that you make every effort to meet the deadlines set, both for first submissions and resubmissions, because otherwise you may find work piling up towards the end of the course.

Fulfilling requirements

It is very important that you actually do what you are asked to do in the assignment. When you have drafted your assignment, check the wording of the task to ensure that you have included all the components required. Two of the main reasons that trainees are asked to resubmit their assignments is because they have not followed the instructions carefully enough, or have left out one or more parts of the assignment.

Relevance

Although 3000–4000 words may sound a lot, that is for all four assignments. Each assignment is generally 750 to 1000 words long, though this may be different at your centre. You will probably find it a challenge to include all you want to say in the number of words you have for each assignment. It is therefore important that you write concisely and include only relevant information.

Look at the following extract from the *Focus on the learner* assignment. Can you identify two sentences which are probably not directly related to Cinzia's needs as an English learner?

> Cinzia lives in a small town in the north of Italy, Saronno. Saronno is famous for the production of a drink called 'Amaretto', although Cinzia herself is not keen on it. Cinzia is a doctor and she combines a busy professional life with bringing up her two children (Eugenia, 9, and Carlo, 7). She learned a little English at school, but says she was easily bored and preferred maths and science subjects. As a doctor she needs to be able to read medical journals, which are often published in English, and one of her motivations for learning English is to allow her to do this. She also attends conferences and would like to develop some 'social conversation skills'. When not working or studying, Cinzia likes to watch her favourite football team, AC Milan, and she tries to attend at least three or four matches a season.

Detail

Although it is important to only include relevant information, you also need to include detail where necessary. In the *Focus on the learner* assignment, for example, you may well be asked to include a reference to specific material to help the learner with an identified difficulty.

Compare these two responses:

> Jurgen wishes to improve his grammar, so something from *English Grammar in Use* Intermediate (Murphy, Cambridge) would be appropriate.

> Jurgen wishes to improve his grammar. I noticed in my conversations with him that he made several errors using reported speech (see transcript on page 7), and so I would recommend *English Grammar in Use* Intermediate 5th edition (Murphy, Cambridge) Unit 47 (page 94), which deals with this and provides practice that he could do outside class time.

Accuracy of information

It is important that what you write is accurate. Here is part of a *Language related tasks* assignment.

Analyse the form and meaning of the underlined parts of the sentences. Suggest a context in which the sentence could be introduced. In each case say how you would check understanding. You do not need to write in complete sentences.

1 <u>Would you like</u> *an ice cream?*

2 <u>Are you going</u> *on holiday next week?*

Now look at a trainee's response. Consider the accuracy and detail of the work and then grade it as 'Pass' or 'Needs resubmission'.

---

1 *Would you like an ice cream?*

  Would + subject + verb

  Used to make offers.

  Context: parent to a child

  Checking: I'd ask questions.

2 *Are you going on holiday next week?*

  going to future

  talking about the future

  Context: in a restaurant

  Checking: I'd ask questions

Now look at another trainee's response. Again, grade the work as 'Pass' or 'Needs resubmission', according to the accuracy and detail.

---

1 *Would you like an ice cream?*

  would + subject + base form of the verb

  Used to make an offer

  Context: parent to a child, standing by an ice-cream van on a hot day. I might introduce this with a picture in a lesson. Clearly the child should not be holding an ice-cream.

  Checking: I'd ask a question such as:

  'Is this about one time, now, or something that the child always likes?' (one time)

2 *Are you going on holiday next week?*

  present continuous (question form *be* + subject + present participle)

  Used to talk about future plans/arrangements

  Context: two colleagues talking

  Checking: I'd ask questions such as:

  'Is the holiday planned or not planned?' (planned)

  'Do you think he has booked his hotel already?' (probably, yes)

Standard of written English

As a teacher you will have to teach writing skills. It is therefore important that you demonstrate your ability to write accurately in terms of spelling, grammar and linking. Even if you meet the other criteria for the assignment, you may be asked to resubmit if the level of accuracy of your writing makes it challenging to read.

Look at the following piece of writing taken from the *Lessons from the classroom* assignment. Do you think it is of an appropriate standard for a teacher of English?

> When I start teaching I knew that my writting on the board was not great – not at all. The tutor told me in the first lesson that it was a bit iffy but I tried for the next lesson. There's alot of things to learn when you start teaching because there's grammer, vocabulary and skills. I was maybe thinking too much about all of them things to really be able to do myself justice.

5-minute activities

Many teachers find it useful to a have a bank of short activities that they can use during lessons. These short activities are often referred to as 'warmers' or 'fillers'. They can be useful to change the pace of the lesson, to help learners relax, to help build the dynamics of the group and to give variety. They are often used at the start of lessons, but they can be exploited at any point in a lesson to help to improve the quality of the activity that follows, for example by building energy prior to a quieter, more reflective, task.

Some warmers have a clear linguistic element (such as vocabulary revision) but others have a more affective purpose. Many can be done either as a whole-class activity or in small groups. The teacher needs to assess the appropriacy of these short activities. Some groups enjoy and benefit from them, while others may feel that they are a block to focusing on the main point of the lesson.

Most of the activities described below can be used in either a physical classroom or online, with only minor changes in how they are set up.

Getting to know you

My name is ... and I like ...

A memory game. Go round the class: the first person completes the formula *My name is ... and I like ...* . The next person reports this (*Her name is ... and she likes ... .*) and then adds their own name and something they like, and so on, each person reporting on what everyone else has said, before adding something new.

Five-pointed star

Learners each draw a five-pointed star. On the first point they write a person's name that is important to them; on the second a place name; on the third a number; on the fourth a date; and on the fifth a sign, symbol or logo. They then get into pairs or small groups, show each other their stars, and ask and answer questions about them.

Phonemic likes and dislikes

Display the following questions in phonemic script:
- Who's your favourite actor?
- What kind of music do you like?
- What was the last video game you played?

Learners write their answers in phonemic script. They then share their answers with each other and comment on them.

Maps

Face-to-face: The learners imagine the room as a world map (establish north, south, east and west, and where one country is on the 'map'). They must then go and stand on the country they would most like to visit and talk to others who are near them about why they have chosen that part of the world.

Online: ask learners to place a cross onto a slide of a world map and then discuss their choice with other learners.

Last weekend

In pairs learners ask and answer yes/no questions in order to find out as much as possible about their partner's weekend. They then report to the class.

In a line

Ask learners to organize themselves either physically into a line (in a classroom), or to write their names in the correct sequence (online), according to specific criteria, e.g. birthday, distance they travel to get to the centre, number of foreign countries visited, alphabetical order of first (given) name, etc.

What I like about you is ...

Learners work in small groups. One member of the group in turn should remain silent while the other members have 30 seconds to pay as many compliments as they can to that person, beginning *What I like about you is ...* .

Word games

What word?

The teacher gives a word to a learner, who must then represent the word either through drawing a picture or through mime. Others guess the word. This can be played as a team game. If preferred, learners can select the words themselves.

Kim's game

The teacher collects seven or eight possessions from members of the class (with their permission) and then covers them. The learners must remember what items were collected and who they belonged to.

Online, every learner holds a possession up to the camera simultaneously for a specified period of time, then puts it out of shot. The learners must remember who held up what.

Vocabulary quiz

The teacher prepares a short quiz with questions such as:
* *Think of five things that are green.*
* *Think of three things that are thinner than a pencil.*
* *Think of six things you could keep money in.*

The teacher allows two minutes for the learners to write answers after each question. Learners can play individually or in small groups. Learners report back answers when the quiz is complete.

Letters to words

The teacher gives the class a collection of letters. Learners have to form as many words as they can, using each letter only once.

Alphabet game

The teacher gives the class (or groups) a topic, e.g. *transport* or *cinema*. The learners have to think of words beginning with as many letters of the alphabet as they can that they associate with the topic.

I went to the market …

Each learner adds an element to the formula: *I went to the market and I bought …* and repeats from memory what other learners said. Variants: *I went to the pharmacy / stationers / clothing department …*; *For my summer holiday, I packed …*

Relaxing

Visualization

Everyone should close their eyes. Play the class a piece of relaxing music. As it plays, tell the class a story, or engage them in creating the story by asking questions as they listen. So, for example, the teacher could either say: *You see a beautiful sailing boat on the horizon, with a bright yellow sail* or *You see a boat on the horizon. What does it look like?*

The learners do not say anything until after the story is finished, when they can share their thoughts.

If I were

The teacher displays some *If I were* sentence stems and the learners complete them and then compare their answers. For example:

If I were a season, I'd be … because …

If I were a colour, I'd be … because …

Classroom quiz

Everyone except one person should close their eyes. That person then asks simple questions about either the physical environment, or, if online, what can be seen in the camera shot e.g. *How many windows are in the room?*.

Paper conversation

Learners work in pairs or small groups, and share one piece of paper, or type on a shared document. On this they ask and answer questions, as if they were having a conversation, but writing – not speaking.

Teach a Martian

The teacher poses as an alien and asks the class to tell him/her how to boil an egg. This will involve explaining what an egg is, a chicken, a bird, etc.

> *Alien:*   *How do I boil an egg?*
> *Learner 1:* *You need a saucepan of water.*
> *Alien:*   *Excellent – thanks. But what is a saucepan?*
> *Learner 2:* *It's a thing you cook food in.*
> *Alien:*   *Oh, yes. Like a microwave – we have those on my planet.*
> *Learner 3:* *No, not a microwave. Can I use the board? I'll draw it.*
> *Etc.*

Once the teacher has modelled it, learners can work in small groups to do the same activity.

Energy raising

Yes/No game

One person must answer yes/no questions asked by others, and must do so without saying *yes* or *no*.

Finding a partner

The teacher distributes halves of sentences, questions and answers, infinitives and past forms, or anything else where there is a clear 'partner'. The learners must mingle and try to find their partner.

My word, your word

Learners work in pairs and must answer questions asked by the rest of the group. However, they are only allowed to say one word at a time, and so must listen to each other to try to form utterances that make sense and are grammatically accurate.

For example: Question: *What is your favourite time of day?*

> A: My
> B: favourite
> A: time
> B: is
> and so on.

How do you feel?

Learners must have short conversations in which they greet each other, but every few seconds the teacher 'changes their mood' by saying, for example, *Say it as if you are exhausted, Say it as if you have just received some really good news, Say it as if you are speaking to a former boyfriend/girlfriend,* etc. (In an online environment the teacher can broadcast messages to the group.)

Physical exercise

The teacher gives instructions to the class to do a (very light) physical workout. For example:

Teacher: Stand up, and copy me. Do what I do. All stretch as high as you can. And bend – try to touch your toes. Walk on the spot. Like me – get your knees high.

Find something ...

Create a short list of criteria or ask the learners to create one. Learners have 3 minutes to find as many of the things as they can. This can be used to practise various language points or vocabulary sets. For example: *Find something round/square/triangular, Find something which you use to write/which you find at school/which you can put in your pocket.*

Mini-conversation

Learners have a conversation in pairs, but each utterance can only be a maximum of two words long, said with the appropriate intonation. For example:

    A: Last night?
    B: TV.
    A: Interesting?
    B: Boring ...

Who am I?

Attach sticky notes with the names of famous people to learners' foreheads, so they can't see whose name it is. They all circulate, asking and answering questions, e.g. *Am I a film star? Am I American?*, until they have guessed who they are.

Last lesson

Learners write three things that are true about the last lesson and two that are untrue. They then read them out, and others have to say whether they are true or not.

For example, *Alejandra was speaking Spanish when the teacher came in.*

A brief guide to the English verb

Verbs can be affirmative (She speaks three languages), negative (She doesn't speak Japanese) or in a question form (Does she speak Italian?).

1 Negation: to negate a verb form, insert 'not' ('nt) after the first auxiliary. *It isn't raining. The children haven't been studying.* In the absence of an auxiliary, insert the appropriate form of 'do' and add 'not' ('nt): *It doesn't work. My parents didn't approve.*

2 Question forms: to make a question, invert the subject and first auxiliary: *Is it raining? Have the children been studying?* In the absence of an auxiliary, invert the subject with an appropriate form of 'do': *Does it work? Did your parents approve?*

Present simple

Examples:

He usually drives to work.
The sun rises in the east.
I don't eat meat.
What time does your train leave?

Uses:

to talk about routines and habits
to talk about things that are always true
to talk about schedules and timetables

Form:

base form of the verb (+ *s* in the third person singular)

Past simple

Examples:

He played for England in the 1970s.
We didn't see them.
When did you wake up?

Uses:

to talk about completed actions in the past

Form:

base form + *ed* (for regular verbs)

Future with *will*

Examples:

You won't win the lottery.
We'll drop by later.
The President will meet the PM on Tuesday.

Uses:

to make predictions about the future
to express decisions made at the time of speaking
to give facts about the future

Form:

will + base form of the verb

Future with *going to*

Examples:

She's going to look for a new job.
Are you going to see Juliet later?
It's not going to snow tomorrow.

Uses:

to talk about plans
to make predictions about the future

Form:

be + *going to* + base form of the verb

Present continuous/progressive

Examples:

He's playing upstairs at the moment.
The universe is expanding.
What time are we meeting?

Uses:

to talk about actions in progress in the present
to describe changes in progress in the present
to talk about future plans and arrangements

Form:

am/is/are + present participle

Past continuous/progressive

Examples:

They were having dinner at the Mermaid Inn when we saw them.
Where were they going?

Uses:

to talk about an action in progress at (and perhaps after) another point in time in the past

Form:

was/were + present participle

Future continuous

Examples:

I'll be working all day tomorrow.
Message her now – she'll be watching the cricket.
He'll be meeting the PM later today.

Uses:

to talk about things happening around a point of time in the future
to talk about planned future events
to make predictions about things happening at the time of speaking

Form:

will + *be* + present participle

Present perfect simple

Examples:

Have you seen Casablanca?
They've lived in the same house for years.
I've fed the cats.

Uses:

to talk about a past situation at an unspecified time that has present relevance
to talk about something started in the past and continuing to the present
to talk about a recently completed action that has present consequences

Form:

have/has + past participle

Past perfect simple

Examples:

She had decided to leave him before we met.
Had you known each other long before you got married?

Use:

to sequence past actions

Form:

had + past participle

Future perfect simple

Examples:

They'll have been married for three years in June.
Some types of frog will have become extinct by 2050.
He'll have arrived by now, I expect.

Uses:

to say how long something will have been in progress by a point in the future
to say that something will be finished before a particular point in time
to make predictions about things happening at the time of speaking

Form:

will + *have* + past participle

Present perfect continuous/ progressive

She's been commuting for years.
Have you been working all night?
What have you been doing?

Uses:

to talk about something started in the past and continuing to the present
to talk about recently completed actions (particularly if there is some evidence)

Form:

have/has + *been* + present participle

Past perfect continuous

Examples:

We had been playing there for ages before anyone complained.
I hadn't been looking to change my job, but this offer was too good to turn down.

Use:

to talk about situations in progress prior to a specific point in the past.

Form:

had + *been* + present participle

Future perfect continuous/ progressive

Examples:

By next month, he'll have been running marathons for fourteen years.
How long will we have been dating by October?

Use:

to say how long something will have been in progress up to a point in the future

Form:

will + *have* + *been* + present participle

Glossary

accent the influence of a person's social, geographical and first language background on their pronunciation.

accuracy the extent to which a learner's use of a second language conforms to a standard form of that language; it is often contrasted with **fluency.**

acquisition the process of language development in an individual; it is sometimes used to mean the natural process of picking up a language, in contrast to learning, which involves formal instruction.

active listening when a listener shows that they are paying attention to a speaker, for example by nodding their head or asking follow-up questions.

active (voice) a verb form such as *makes* or *was writing* where the **subject** is the person doing the action, as compared to the **passive** (*is made, was written*).

adjective a word, such as *old, blue* or *interesting,* that tells you about the qualities of a person or thing or event.

adverb a word, such as *quickly, well, here* or *then,* which tells you about the circumstances of an event, such as how or where or when it happens.

affirmative (sentence) a sentence that makes a positive statement, as opposed to a negative one.

affix an element that is added either to the beginning of a word (in the case of **prefixes,** such as *un-, anti-, re-*) or to the end of the word (in the case of **suffixes,** such as *–less, -wise, -ly*), and which change the word's meaning or **part of speech.**

aim the learning objective of a teaching sequence; a distinction is made between the **main** or primary aim and secondary or **subsidiary** aims; aims are defined in terms of linguistic items, such as verb forms, and also in terms of **skills** development; or in terms of communicative outcome.

antonym a word, such as *old,* which is opposite in meaning to another word, such as *young* or *new.*

appropriacy, appropriateness the use of language that is suitable for its context, e.g. not too formal in an informal context.

article either of the **determiners** *the* (definite article) or *a/an* (indefinite article) as in *the banana, a banana;* when nouns are used without an article, the absence of the article is called zero article: *it tastes like banana.*

aspect a verb form that expresses the speaker's view of the event described by the verb, such as whether it is in progress, or complete. There are two aspects in English: **continuous** (also **progressive**) and **perfect**.

assessment collecting information in order to gauge a learner's progress; assessment may be formal, as in **testing,** or informal, as in simply observing learners doing tasks.

asynchronous (teaching/learning) lessons which happen online with the teacher and learner(s) accessing the course at their own pace, for example via recordings or forums, in contrast to **synchronous**. There is no real-time interaction.

authentic materials classroom materials that were not originally written or spoken for language teaching purposes, such as news articles or television documentaries.

authentic task an activity which reflects what would happen in an authentic situation outside the classroom. For example, note-taking while listening to a lecture is an authentic task, whereas answering true or false questions is probably not.

auxiliary verb grammar words such as *do, had, was,* that are used with **main verbs** to form tenses, questions, and negatives.

bare infinitive the **infinitive** form without *to,* as in *she made me <u>do</u> it.*

base form (of the verb) the form of the verb that is not inflected by the addition of grammatical elements, such as *–ing, -ed, -s*, for example *go* or *drink*.

bottom-up knowledge familiarity with the words and grammatical structures in a spoken or written text, which interacts with **top-down knowledge,** e.g. of topic or text type, to aid comprehension.

CEFR (Common European Framework of Reference) a project aimed at providing a common basis for language education in Europe, in such areas as **syllabus** design and **assessment**, and consisting of a description of the components of language proficiency at all levels and across a range of skills.

checking understanding the process of gauging the learners' grasp of a new concept, by asking **concept (checking) questions,** for example.

chunk (also **multi-word unit)** a phrase of two or more words that is stored and used as a single unit, such as *by the way, head over heels, see you later.*

classroom management the ways the teacher organizes and controls the classroom activity, including the learners' interactions and the use of resources.

clause a group of words containing a **verb**, forming the main structures of which sentences are built: *[She was sitting in the waiting-room], [reading a newspaper], [when it was announced [that the train [she was waiting for] had been delayed]].*

CLIL (content and language integrated learning) the use of a language other than the learners' **L1** to teach a school subject such as science or physical education, with the aim of developing competence in both the target language and specified subject.

cloze test a test consisting of a text in which every *n*th word has been replaced by a space.

coherence the capacity of a spoken or written text to make sense to the listener/reader because of the way it is organized, for example.

cohesion the way in which the units of a text (the words, clauses, and sentences) are meaningfully connected, through the use of cohesive devices such as **linkers.**

collocation the way that certain words regularly occur together, such as *good clean fun,* but not *bad dirty fun.*

communicative activity a classroom speaking or writing task in which the learners have to interact in order to solve a problem or complete a task.

communicative aim → aim

communicative approaches language teaching methods whose goal is meaningful communication rather than knowledge of language rules, for example.

comparative the form of an adjective or adverb that is used to make comparisons: *older, better, more expensive, less often.*

compound noun a noun formed from two or more individual words, such as *bookshop, hairdryer, washing machine.*

concept the basic meaning of a word or structure, independent of context, e.g. *You can go now.* means *You are free to go now.*

concept (checking) questions (or **CCQs**) one method of **concept** checking, in which the teachers asks questions in order to check the learners' understanding of a new word or grammar structure.

conditional the form of a verb made with *would/should*: *I would ask someone;* a conditional clause is one that usually starts with *if,* which tells us about possible or hypothetical situations: *If you don't know a word, look it up. I would ask someone, if I were you.*

conjunction a word such as *and, but, so,* that links two **clauses**, or phrases, or words.

connected speech the way that speech sounds are produced as part of a continuous sequence, rather than in isolation.

consonant in pronunciation, a sound that is made when the airflow from the lungs is obstructed in some way, such as /b/, /p/ or /v/.

content words (also known as lexical words) the words in a text which carry the main information load; for example *I'm living in Poland at the moment,* in contrast to the **grammar words**. Content words are usually **nouns, adjectives, main verbs** or **adverbs.**

context either the text that immediately surrounds a language item (also called co-text), or the particular situation in which language is used (also called context of situation).

continuous/progressive (aspect) the **aspect** of the verb that is formed by combining the **auxiliary verb** *be* with the **present participle**: *She is leaving. It was raining.*

continuing professional development (CPD) the act of continuing to develop as a teacher throughout your career, both through external stimuli like reading or attending workshops, and internal stimuli like reflection.

contraction the reduction of some elements that results in joining two words, such as a **pronoun** (*they, it*) and an **auxiliary verb** (*will, is*): *they'll, it's.*

controlled practice (sometimes called **restricted practice**) a stage in the teaching of a language item in which the learners use the item in restricted contexts so as to gain mastery of the form, rather than to use the item communicatively; **drilling** is a form of controlled practice.

corpus (pl. **corpora**) a digital database of texts that can be used to research how language is actually used.

countable noun a noun such as *day, child* or *glass*, that refers to something that can be counted, and so has a plural form: *days, children, glasses;* uncountable nouns, like *water* or *information*, do not normally have plural forms.

coursebook (also called **textbook**) the book that contains the materials used in a language course, often part of a series, each part aimed at one level.

deductive learning an approach to learning where learners are given rules which they then apply in the creation of examples; it contrasts with **inductive learning.**

determiner a word, such as *the, some, my, many, no,* etc. that belongs to the class of words that can go at the beginning of a **noun phrase**: *the woman in white; my many friends.*

Determiners help to identify things (e.g. if the thing is known or unknown to the hearer) or to quantify things: *All the staff went on strike.*

differentiation adapting materials or activities to the level, learning dispositions and special needs of individual learners.

diphthong a **vowel** sound, such as the ones in *boy* and *cow*, that is made when the tongue changes position mid-sound to produce a sound like two vowels joined together.

discourse any connected piece of speech or writing; the analysis of its connectedness is called discourse analysis.

display question a question asked by a teacher in order for learners to display their knowledge. For example, *What tense is this?*, in contrast to a **real question**.

drill, drilling a form of **controlled practice** involving oral repetition of words or sentence patterns. Drilling can be **choral**, when the whole class (or a section of the class) is repeating the item together, or **individual.**

dynamic verb a verb which expresses an event or activity, such as *run* or *eat*, and which can therefore be used in the **continuous aspect**, in contrast to **stative verbs.**

EAP (English for Academic Purposes) the teaching of English to students who will need to use English in their studies, particularly for university study.

educational technology (also **edtech**) the use, or design, of technology, particularly software, to aid teaching and learning.

EFL (English as a Foreign Language) the learning of English in a context where English is not generally the medium of communication. For example, this would include a Japanese student having English classes in Japan.

EIL (English as an International Language) the use of English as a means of communication between speakers of different L1s; also called English as a lingua franca (ELF). For example, a Mandarin speaker and a Swahili speaker speaking together in English.

ELF (English as a lingua franca) → **EIL**

eliciting the teacher's use of questions, or other prompts, to get learners to provide answers and responses, often with the intention of finding out what they already know.

ellipsis the omission of an otherwise obligatory element in a sentence because it can be inferred from the context: [THERE IS A] RAILROAD CROSSING AHEAD.

engagement the degree to which learners are actively participating in and interested in (parts of) the lesson, which in turn may affect their attitude to, and enjoyment of, learning.

ESL (English as a Second Language) the teaching of English to speakers of other languages who live in a country where English is an official or important language.

ESP (English for Specific Purposes, also **English for Special Purposes)** a general term for the content of courses that are targeted at groups of learners whose particular vocational or academic needs have been identified, such as businesspeople or medical professionals; EAP is one example of ESP.

extensive reading the reading of longer texts, such as stories or novels, in order to gain a general, not detailed, understanding, and often for pleasure.

feedback the messages that learners get about their language use or their language learning; positive feedback is information that the learner's language use has been correct; negative feedback indicates that it has been incorrect.

finger correction, finger coding the use of the fingers to represent the elements of a word or phrase in order to display its form or to identify an error.

flashcard a card with pictures or words on it which is used as a prompt in the lesson.

fluency the capacity to be communicative in real-time conditions; often contrasted with **accuracy**.

focus on form a stage in teaching where the learner's attention is directed to the form of a language item, e.g. when the teacher points out the *–ed* ending on regular past tense verbs.

form the way that words or structures are spoken or written, e.g. /miːt/ is written as *meat* or *meet*; the past of *meet* is *met*.

formulaic expression a conventionalized way of expressing a **concept** or **function**. For example, *Would you like [an X]?* typically functions as an offer.

function the communicative purpose of a language item, often described in terms of speech acts, such as *offering, apologizing, requesting, asking for information*.

functional exponent one of the ways that a **function** is commonly realized; thus, a functional exponent of *offering* is *Would you like …?*

gap-fill an exercise that requires learners to complete a sentence or text in which certain items have been removed.

genre any type of spoken or written **discourse** which is used and recognized by members of a particular culture or sub-culture.

gerund the form of the verb ending in *-ing*, and which acts like a noun, as in *No parking*; the term *-ing* **form** is now more generally used. See also the **present participle**.

gist a general understanding of a written or spoken text, as opposed to a detailed understanding; a gist task is one that checks or tests this general understanding.

graded reader an extended reading text where the level of language has been controlled so as to be more easily intelligible for learners, often used as part of **extensive reading**.

grading (language) the way teachers simplify their classroom language in the interests of intelligibility, especially with beginners and elementary learners.

grammar the process by which language is organized and patterned in order to make meaning, and also the description of the rules that govern this process.

grammar words the closed set of words which express grammatical relationships between **content words**: *I'm living in Poland at the moment.*

guided discovery a form of inductive learning in which learners are encouraged to work out rules for themselves, with some teacher guidance.

head word the main word in a **phrase**, which tells you what kind of phrase it is. For example, in *a black cat*, the noun *cat* is the head, making it a noun phrase.

highlighting (form) techniques that draw learners' attention to the forms of second language items, such as using boardwork to show inversion in question forms.

homophone a word that sounds like another word, but is written differently, such as *sea* and *see*. A **homograph** is spelt the same as another word, but pronounced differently, as in *the long and windy road; a dark and windy night*. A **homonym** is the same in both spelling and pronunciation as another word, but different in meaning, as in *a cricket bat* and *a vampire bat*.

idiom a phrase whose meaning is not literal, and is not deducible from its components, as in *a can of worms* (= *a complicated problem*).

imperative the **base form** of the verb when it is used without a subject to give instructions, orders or directions: *Turn left. Don't say that.*

indirect question a question that is embedded in a statement or another question, as in *I don't know what her name is. Can you tell me when the bank opens?*

inductive learning an approach to learning in which learners are given examples of a structure and they then work out the rules underlying them; it contrasts with **deductive learning**.

infinitive the **base form** of the verb, used with or without *to* (in the latter case it is called the **bare infinitive),** as in *to be or not to be; you made me love you*. When the infinitive expresses an intention it is called the **infinitive of purpose**: *We stopped to admire the view.*

information gap a type of **communicative activity** in which the information that is necessary in order to complete a task is distributed between the two or more learners who are doing the task, so that they must communicate with one another.

-ing form a word ending in *–ing*, such as *cooking* or *seeing*, which is used 1) to form verb tenses where it is also called the **present participle**: *I'm cooking.* and 2) like a noun after certain verbs and prepositions where it is also called a **gerund**: *I like cooking. I look forward to seeing you.*

integrated skills the teaching of the **skills** (of reading, writing, speaking and listening) in conjunction with one another, rather than separately, for example watching a video and then writing a comment about it.

intelligibility how possible it is to understand the speech or writing of a particular person.

interaction the use of language between people; interaction is considered a necessary condition for language **acquisition**.

interaction pattern the way in which learners are grouped (or not) in order to complete an activity, for example alone, in pairs, or in two teams.

interactive listening listening as part of, for example, a conversation, in which the listener has to both process what they hear and formulate a response, in contrast to **non-interactive listening**.

interlanguage the grammatical system that a learner creates in the course of learning another language.

intonation the use of either rising or falling pitch in speech to contribute to meaning.

intransitive verb a verb, such as *laugh, go, happen*, that doesn't take an **object**: *nobody laughed; something happened*.

irregular verb a verb such as *go, say, or write*, whose **past simple** form and/or **past participle** does not end in *-ed*.

jigsaw technique a type of **communicative activity** in which information is distributed among the members of a group, so that, in order to complete a task, they must share the information.

L1 the learner's first language(s), or mother tongue(s).

L2 the learner's second (or possibly third, or fourth, etc.) language, which, when it is the object of instruction, is also called the **target language**.

learner autonomy the capacity of the learner to learn independently of teachers, and one of the goals of **learner training**.

learner dictionary a dictionary written specifically for language learners, for example the *Cambridge Advanced Learner's Dictionary*. It uses a limited range of defining vocabulary, and may contain other information to help learners, such as potentially confusing words.

learner training techniques that help learners make the most of learning opportunities, such as ways of recording and memorizing incidental vocabulary.

learning preferences the learner's preferred ways of approaching learning, influenced by their personality or by their previous learning experience, for example working in groups, or learning grammar by reading rules.

learning strategies techniques or behaviours that learners consciously apply in order to improve their learning, such as asking the meaning of unfamiliar words.

lexical approach an approach to language teaching that foregrounds the importance of vocabulary acquisition, including the learning of **chunks.**

lexical set a group of words that are thematically related, such as *windscreen, steering wheel, handbrake, indicator.*

lexis the vocabulary of a language, as opposed to its **grammar.**

linguistic aim → aim

linkers (also **cohesive devices**) words, such as *but, nevertheless, therefore,* which are used to connect ideas within texts.

literacy the ability to read and write in a language.

main aim → aim

main verb the lexical **verb** in a complex verb **phrase** that combines with one or more **auxiliary verbs**: *Kim has arrived. It must have been raining.*

mastery having complete control over one's use of the (target) language.

materials evaluation the act of deciding to what extent a specific set of materials might be appropriate for a specific learning and teaching context; generally based on pre-defined criteria.

metalanguage the language that is used to talk about language, such as grammatical terminology.

milling, mingling an activity in which learners move around the classroom space and interact with one another in turn, as when conducting a survey, for example.

minimal pair a pair of words which differ in meaning when only one sound is changed, such as *bin* and *bean,* or *ban* and *pan.*

modal verb a verb, such as *can, may, should, must,* which is used to express possibility and to make offers, suggestions, commands, etc. To form questions and negatives, modal verbs function like **auxiliary verbs**, as they combine directly with main verbs.

model sentence a sentence, often taken from a longer text, which is used as an example of a particular grammar **structure** for teaching purposes.

model text a written example of a particular type of text which learners can imitate.

monitoring the process of observing learners doing a **task** in order to check that they are 'on task', to collect samples of language to give feedback on, to collect information about learner performance in activities, and to be available for consultation.

monophthong a **vowel** sound, such as the ones in *cat* and *egg,* that is made without any movement of the tongue, lips, etc from one position to another, in contrast to a **diphthong**.

motivation the effort that learners put into language learning as a result of their desire or need to learn the language.

multi-word unit → chunk

needs analysis the process of determining the purposes for which a learner is learning a language, used to design a course (typically an **ESP** course) that is appropriate.

nominating indicating which learner is to answer a question by using their name, or through using a gesture.

non-interactive listening listening to, for example, a podcast, in which the listener simply listens without having to speak, in contrast to **interactive listening**.

noun a word, such as *bus, driver, journey, fare, request,* etc. that names things. They can be used after a **determiner** and as the **subject** or **object** of a sentence.

noun phrase a word or group of words consisting of at least a **noun** or a **pronoun** and which functions like a noun: *last night; your old car; I; those big red London buses.*

object a **noun phrase** which refers to what or who is affected by the action described by the verb: *I caught the bus. I paid the driver* (= indirect object) *the fare* (= direct object).

objective test a test that can be marked without requiring the test marker's personal judgement, as opposed to a **subjective test.**

observation noticing what another teacher (or yourself in the case of self-observation) does in the classroom in order to learn from it, to help that teacher to develop (developmental observation) or to assess their teaching abilities (evaluative observation).

pace the flow of activities in a lesson, and the (perceived) variations in the speed and intensity of the activities.

part of speech (also **word class**) any one of the (usually) eight classifications of words according to their function, i.e. **noun, verb, adjective, adverb, determiner, pronoun, preposition** and **conjunction.**

passive (voice) a verb form, such as *is made* or *was written,* where the **subject** is the person or thing who is affected by the action, as compared to the **active** (*makes, was writing*).

past continuous (or progressive) the form of the verb that combines the past of the **auxiliary verb** *be* with the present participle: *It was raining. The dogs were barking.*

past participle a verb form that is used to form the **present perfect** and the **passive**: *I have worked. The letter was written.* Regular past participles end in *-ed.*

past perfect the form of the verb that combines the past of the **auxiliary verb** *have* and the past participle: *The film had started.* The form '*had + been + **present participle***' is called the past perfect continuous (or progressive): *It had been raining.*

past simple the form of the verb that takes an *-ed* ending (for **regular verbs**) and typically expresses past meaning: *Dan called. I sent you an e-mail.*

peer correction the correcting of one learner's error by another learner.

perfect (aspect) the **aspect** of the verb that combines the **auxiliary verb** *have* with the **past participle**: *The post has arrived. It had been raining.*

personalization the classroom use of language to express one's own feelings, experiences and thoughts.

phoneme any one of the distinctive sounds of a particular language; for example, standard British English has 44 phonemes, distributed between 24 **consonants** and 20 **vowels.**

phonemic chart a teaching aid that displays the 44 **phonemes** of English in the form of **phonemic script.**

phonemic script the conventional way of representing the **phonemes** of a language; in phonemic script the word *phoneme* is written /ˈfəʊniːm/.

phonology the system of pronunciation of a specific language, and the study of this system.

phrasal verb a **verb** that is made up of two (or sometimes three) parts and which often has idiomatic meaning: *I got up at nine. Do you take after your Dad?*

phrase a meaningful group of words which form a single unit, clustered around a **head word**, either a **noun, verb, adjective, adverb** or **preposition.**

possessive 's' the use of an apostrophe and *s* at the end of a **noun** to indicate ownership: *Claire's knee; the neighbours' cat.*

possessive adjective a word, such as *my, your, her, their,* that precede **nouns** and denote possession: *my bike; your turn.*

possessive pronoun a word, such as *mine, yours, hers, theirs,* that stands for a **noun** and denotes possession: *That bike is mine. Whose turn is it? Yours.*

post-modification words which appear after the **head word** in a **noun phrase.**

PPP (presentation, practice, production)
a format for the staging of grammar (or vocabulary) teaching that starts with the presentation of a new grammar item, followed by **controlled practice,** and ends with free production.

prefix → affix

pre-listening task the task set in advance of listening to a text, often oriented to the **gist** of the text.

pre-modification words which appear before the **head word** in a **noun phrase.**

preposition a word, or group of words, such as *in, on, behind, in front of,* which often indicates place or time, and is always followed by a **noun phrase:** *in the garden; on Sunday; behind the times.*

preselection a method of teaching in which the teacher decides what specific language items to focus on before the lesson rather than during it, as opposed to **teaching reactively**. It is often connected to working with coursebooks.

present continuous (or **progressive**) the form of the verb that combines the present of the **auxiliary verb** *be* with the **present participle**: *It is raining. The doors are opening.*

present participle an *-ing* word that is used to express verbal meaning: *Jan is sleeping. I heard the dog barking.* as compared to a **gerund.**

present perfect the form of the verb that combines the present of the **auxiliary verb** *have* with the **past participle**: *I have phoned for a taxi. Has Kim had lunch?*

present perfect continuous (or **progressive**) the form of the verb that combines the present of the **auxiliary verb** *have* with the **past participle** of *be* and the **present participle**: *It has been snowing; Have you been waiting long?*

present simple the form of the verb that has no **auxiliary verb** and in the third person singular, takes **third person –s**: *They live in Houston. Her back hurts.*

presentation the stage of a lesson where a new language item, such as a grammar structure or a set of vocabulary, is introduced.

process writing an approach to the teaching of writing that emphasizes the composing processes rather than the finished product.

productive skills the skills of speaking and writing, in contrast to the **receptive skills**.

progressive → continuous

project-based lessons lessons focused on the individual or collaborative production of a piece of work that usually involves some out-of-class research and preparation, and which is then presented, either in spoken or written form, or a combination of the two, as opposed to a lesson which focuses primarily on language work.

pronoun a word such as *she, me, it, you,* etc., that can be used in place of a **noun** as **subject** or **object** of a sentence.

pronunciation the way the sounds of a language are spoken.

quantifier words or phrases which specify quantity or amount, e.g. *all, a few of, loads of.*

question tag a structure containing an **auxiliary verb** and a **pronoun,** which is added to a sentence to make a question, as in *It's a nice day, isn't it? You're not hungry, are you?*

rapport the feeling of mutual understanding and respect that exists between learners and their teacher.

real question a question asked by a teacher when they do not know the answer, for example, *What did you do on your holiday?*, in contrast to a **display question**.

realia real objects that are used in the classroom as aids for teaching and learning.

receptive skills the skills of listening and reading, in contrast to the **productive skills**.

recycle/recycling returning to previously studied topics in a later lesson, particularly grammar or vocabulary, in order to help learners to revise or remember them.

reflection the process of thinking about teaching and learning experiences in order to learn from them and improve your own practice in the future.

reflexive pronoun a **pronoun,** such as *myself, himself, themselves,* used when the object of the verb refers to the same person as the subject: *I cut myself.*

reformulation (also known as recasting) a method of error correction in which the teacher repeats what the learner said, but in the correct form, without drawing attention to the error explicitly.

register the way that the use of language varies according to variations in the context, such as the social distance between speakers, or the topic, or the medium.

regular verb a **verb**, such as *work, live, start,* whose past tense and **past participle** are formed by adding *-(e)d* to the **base form:** *worked, lived, started.* **Irregular verbs** do not follow this rule.

relative clause a **clause** that gives more information about something mentioned in the main clause: *This is the house where Freud lived.*

relative pronoun a **pronoun** that connects a **relative clause** to its noun: *This is the house where Freud lived.*

reported speech the way in which the sense of what some has said (but not their exact wording) is incorporated into a text, and where grammatical changes may be introduced: *'I'm hungry' = He said he was hungry.* Also called indirect speech, in contrast to direct speech.

reporting verb a verb, such as *say, tell, ask, wonder,* that is typically used to report speech or thoughts.

rhythm the way that in speech some words are emphasized so as to give the effect of regular beats.

role play a classroom activity in which learners adopt different roles and act out a situation according to these roles.

rubric the set of instructions for an exercise or a test that tells or shows the learners what they have to do.

scaffolding the support, through interaction, provided by a teacher (or materials) to enable learners to complete a task successfully at a level beyond their current competence.

scanning in reading, searching a text for specific information while ignoring other parts of the text, as when a reader searches a film review for the place where the film is set.

scheme of work the teacher's plan for a sequence of lessons.

schwa the weak, unstressed **vowel** sound /ə/, which is the most common sound in English.

self-assessment the process of learners evaluating their own learning progress.

SEN (Special Educational Needs) a difficulty or disability which affects a person's ability to learn, for example when concentration levels are affected by ADHD, or working memory is affected by dyslexia.

skill a way in which language is used, such as speaking or reading, in contrast to language **systems**, such as grammar and vocabulary.

skills-focused aim ➜ **aim**

skimming in reading, getting the main ideas, or **gist**, of a text by reading it rapidly and without attention to detail.

standard English the variety of English that is institutionalized (e.g. in education, print media etc.) in a region.

stative/state verb a **verb**, such as *be* or *know,* which expresses a state rather than an activity and which, therefore, is rarely used with the continuous aspect, in contrast to **dynamic verbs.**

stress the effect of emphasizing certain syllables in speech; the stress pattern in individual words (**word stress**) is generally constant, but the stress in sentences (**sentence stress**) can vary according to what the speaker considers to be given, as opposed to, new information: the latter is typically stressed.

strong form the pronunciation of certain words, such as **auxiliary verbs** and **determiners,** when they are stressed, as in *Yes, I can (/kæn/),* which contrasts to their pronunciation when unstressed (called their **weak form**), e.g. *I can (/kən/) swim.*

structure any language pattern that generates specific instances; generally used to describe grammar items, such as verb forms. For example, the present continuous structure might generate the instances *I'm writing an email. He's shopping.*

subject the **noun phrase** that typically comes before the verb and tells you who or what is the agent or topic of the clause: *Chris caught the bus. The bus was crowded.*

subjective test → objective test

subsidiary aim → aim

subskill a subcategory of one of the language **skills**; for example, inferencing is a subskill of the skill of reading.

substitution the use of a pronoun to replace a word which has previously been mentioned. For example: *I've got a cat. Have you got one too?*

substitution table a way of displaying, in the form of a grid, the way the different elements of a **structure** relate to one another.

suffix → affix

superlative the form of an adjective or adverb that is used to show an extreme or unique quality: *the fastest, the most unusual, the best.*

syllable a unit of pronunciation that is typically larger than a sound but smaller than a word: the word *syllable* has three syllables.

syllabus the selection and sequence of items making up a course. A language syllabus is often organized in terms of grammar **structures**.

synchronous (teaching/learning) generally used to describe lessons which take place online with the teacher and learner(s) present at the same time, for example via a video call, in contrast to **asynchronous**. There is real-time interaction.

synonym a word that has the same meaning as another one, as in *jail* and *prison*.

systems the linguistic constituents of language, such as **grammar**, **vocabulary**, **phonology** and **discourse**, in contrast to the way these constituents are used in specific **skills**.

target form the specific item(s) of grammar or vocabulary which are focused on at a given point in the lesson.

target language the L2 which learners are studying, for example English or French.

task a classroom activity whose focus is on communication, rather than on language practice for its own sake.

task-based learning (TBL) a way of organizing language learning around a syllabus of **tasks** rather than grammar **structures**.

teacher talking time (TTT) the extent to which the teacher dominates the speaking time in class.

teacher's book a guide for the teacher that usually accompanies most **coursebooks**.

teaching reactively an approach to teaching in which the teacher decides what specific language items to focus on in response to the learners' needs during a lesson or a task, as opposed to **preselection**.

tense the verb form which shows whether the speaker is referring to past, present or future. In English, technically, there are only two tenses: present (*they go*), and past (*they went*).

test-teach-test a way of describing lessons that begin with some productive task, which is then followed by instruction that targets areas diagnosed as needing teaching, which is in turn followed by a repeat of the initial task, or a similar task.

testing assessing learners' level or progress, either at the outset of a course (placement testing, diagnostic testing), during a course (progress testing), or at the end of a course (achievement testing).

text a continuous piece of spoken or written language.

third person 's' the ending that is added to the base form of the verb in the present simple when talking about *he, she, it,* etc. *she knows; Tom laughs.*

timeline a visual representation of a grammatical **concept**. There are examples on page 80.

top-down knowledge in **receptive skills** awareness of background information (such as prior knowledge about a topic) which can be used in combination with **bottom-up knowledge** (e.g. of vocabulary and grammar) to aid comprehension, or which can compensate for lack of such knowledge.

transitive verb a **verb**, such as *make, put, take,* that takes an **object**: *We made lunch.*

unvoiced/voiceless sound a consonant sound which is produced without vibrating the vocal cords, such as /p/, /k/, /s/, in contrast to a **voiced sound**.

verb a word or words, such as *worked, has, costs, takes off,* that follows the subject of a clause, and expresses what someone or something does or is.

verb pattern the sentence structure that is determined by the choice of verb. For example, the verb *make* can take the pattern *verb + object + bare infinitive: you made me do it,* whereas the verb *force* takes the pattern *verb + object +* to-*infinitive: you forced me to do* it.

very young learners (VYLs) although the exact age range varies depending on the context, these are typically learners aged around 2–6.

voiced sound a sound which is produced while the vocal cords are vibrating; some consonants, like /b/, /g/, /z/, are voiced; all **vowels** are voiced. In contrast to an **unvoiced sound.**

vowel a sound that is produced without obstruction or constriction of the airflow from the lungs, as opposed to **consonants,** where the airflow is interrupted. For example /æ/ or /ə/.

warmer, warm-up an activity done at the beginning of the lesson to ease the transition into the lesson itself.

weak form → strong form

wh-question a question that begins with a word such as *what, when, why, how,* etc.

while-listening task a task that learners perform while listening to a text, e.g. tracing a route on a map.

workbook a book of activities and exercises that usually accompanies a **coursebook**, often used for homework or self-study.

yes/no question a question that can be answered with either *yes* or *no*: *Are you married? Haven't you had lunch?*

young learners (YLs) although the exact age range varies depending on the context, these are typically learners aged around 7–14.

Further reading

Learners and their contexts

Equal Opportunity and Diversity: The Handbook for Teachers of English, The British Council, 2009

Exploring Psychology in Language Learning and Teaching, Marion Williams, Sarah Mercer and Stephen Ryan, Oxford University Press, 2015

How Languages are Learned (4th edition), Patsy Lightbown and Nina Spada, Oxford University Press, 2013

Learner English (2nd edition), Michael Swan and Bernard Smith (eds.), Cambridge University Press, 2001

Special Educational Needs, Marie Delaney, Oxford University Press, 2016

Classroom teaching

100 Teaching Tips, Penny Ur, Cambridge University Press, 2016

30 Language Teaching Methods, Scott Thornbury, Cambridge University Press, 2017

The Cambridge Guide to Learning English as a Second Language, Anne Burns and Jack C. Richards (eds.), Cambridge University Press, 2018

Engaging Language Learners in Contemporary Classrooms, Sarah Mercer and Zoltán Dörnyei, Cambridge University Press, 2020

Learning Teaching (3rd edition), Jim Scrivener, Macmillan, 2017

Learning to Teach English (2nd edition), Peter Watkins, Delta Publishing, 2014

Listening in the Language Classroom, John Field, Cambridge University Press, 2009

The New A–Z of ELT (2nd edition), Scott Thornbury, Macmillan, 2017

Teaching and Developing Reading Skills, Peter Watkins, Cambridge University Press, 2017

Teaching in Challenging Circumstances, Chris Sowton, Cambridge University Press, 2021

Translation and Own-language Activities, Philip Kerr, Cambridge University Press, 2014

Language awareness

About Language: Tasks for Teachers of English (2nd edition), Scott Thornbury, Cambridge University Press, 2017

Grammar for English Language Teachers (2nd edition), Martin Parrott, Cambridge University Press, 2010

Practical English Usage (4th edition), Michael Swan, Oxford University Press, 2016

Professional development

50 Tips for Teacher Development, Jack C. Richards, Cambridge University Press, 2017

The Cambridge Guide to Second Language Teacher Education, Anne Burns and Jack C. Richards (eds.), Cambridge University Press, 2009

The Developing Teacher, Duncan Foord, Delta Publishing, 2017

Professional Development for Language Teachers, Jack C. Richards and Thomas Farrell, Cambridge University Press, 2005

Useful Websites

Cambridge English Language Learning
https://www.cambridge.org/gb/cambridgeenglish

Modern English Teacher
https://www.modernenglishteacher.com

Humanising Language Teaching
https://www.hltmag.co.uk/

Onestopenglish https://www.onestopenglish.com

Useful Organizations

International Association of Teachers of English as a Foreign Language (IATEFL)
https://www.iatefl.org

Teachers of English to Speakers of Other Languages (TESOL)
https://www.tesol.org

British Council
https://www.teachingenglish.org.uk

Course materials

Unit 4

Goldstein, B. & Jones, C. (2019). *Evolve Level 4 Student's book.* Cambridge: Cambridge University Press, contents page

Redston & Cunningham. (2020). *face2face Upper Intermediate Student's book* 2nd edition. Cambridge: Cambridge University Press, p. 129

Unit 5

Doff, Thaine, et al (2017). *Empower B1+ Student's book* 1st edition Cambridge: Cambridge University Press, pp. 70, 142

Godfrey, Gairns, et al (2017). *Empower B1+ Teacher's book* 1st edition Cambridge: Cambridge University Press, p. 89

Unit 6

Redston & Cunningham (2013*). face2face Intermediate Student's book* 2nd edition. Cambridge: Cambridge University Press, p. 46

Puchta, Stranks, Lewis-Jones (2016). *Think B2 Student's book* Cambridge: Cambridge University Press, p. 99

Unit 8

Baker (2006). *Ship or Sheep? An Intermediate Pronunciation Course* 3rd edition. Cambridge: Cambridge University Press,

Unit 9

Redston & Cunningham (2013). *face2face Intermediate Student's book* 2nd edition. Cambridge: Cambridge University Press, p. 95

Redston & Cunningham (2019). *face2face Pre-intermediate* 2nd edition. Cambridge: Cambridge University Press, p. 61

Unit 10

T Puchta, Stranks, Lewis-Jones (2016). *Think B2 Student's book* Cambridge: Cambridge University Press, p. 45

Unit 12

Goldstein & Jones (2019). *Evolve Level 4 Student's book* Cambridge: Cambridge University Press, pp. 2–3.

Murphy (2019). *English Grammar in Use Intermediate* Cambridge: Cambridge University Press, p. 5

Redston & Cunningham (2020). *face2face Upper Intermediate Student's book* 2nd edition. Cambridge: Cambridge University Press, p. 59

Unit 13

Hendra et al (2019). *Evolve Level 1 Student's book* Cambridge: Cambridge University Press, p. 102

Unit 14

Knight and O'Neil (2002). *Business Explorer 2 Student's book* Cambridge: Cambridge University Press, p. 69

Unit 16

Puchta, Stranks, Lewis-Jones (2016). *Think 1 Student's book* Cambridge: Cambridge University Press, p. 94

Unit 20

Redston & Cunningham (2005). *face2face Pre-intermediate* 1st edition. Cambridge: Cambridge University Press, p. 90

Unit 21

Redston & Cunningham (2013). *face2face Intermediate Student's book* 2nd edition. Cambridge: Cambridge University Press, p. 70

Unit 23

Doff, Thaine, et al (2017). *Empower A2 Student's book* 1st edition Cambridge: Cambridge University Press, p. 77

Unit 26

Puchta, H. Stranks, J. Lewis-Jones, P (2015). *American Think 2* Cambridge pp. 38–39

Tilbury, A. et al (2010) *English Unlimited Elementary* Cambridge: Cambridge University Press, p. 11

Unit 36

Doff, Thaine, et al (2017). *Empower A2 Student's book* 1st edition Cambridge: Cambridge University Press, p. 109

Redston & Cunningham (2013). *face2face Intermediate Student's book* 2nd edition. Cambridge: Cambridge University Press, p. 174

Hendra, Ibbotson & O'Dell (2019). *Evolve Level 1 Student's book.* Cambridge: Cambridge University Press, pp. 99, 115

Hendra, Ibbotson & O'Dell (2019). *Evolve Level 5 Student's book.* Cambridge: Cambridge University Press, pp. 79, 95

Pair and group work

Speck, Rimmer, et al (2019). *Evolve Level 1 Teacher's book.* Cambridge: Cambridge University Press, pp. 202

Acknowledgements

The authors would like to thank Karen Momber and Jo Timerick at Cambridge University Press for their support and guidance throughout the project and also Hugh Moss and his team for their valuable input. Indeed, we are sincerely grateful to all those behind the scenes at Cambridge University Press and Assessment for their contributions to all aspects of this work. Our thanks are also due to David Bunker for his editorial expertise and all those who commented on drafts of the manuscript.

The authors and publishers acknowledge the following sources of copyright material and are grateful for the permissions granted. While every effort has been made, it has not always been possible to identify the sources of all the material used, or to trace all copyright holders. If any omissions are brought to our notice, we will be happy to include the appropriate acknowledgements on reprinting and in the next update to the digital edition, as applicable.

Key: U = Unit, TB = Trainee Book, TM = Trainer's Manual

Text

TB – U4: Ryôkan, ["In the empty doorway many petals are scattered;"] from *One Robe, One Bowl: The Zen Poetry of Ryôkan, translated and introduced by John Stevens*, First edition, 1977. Protected by copyright under the terms of the International Copyright Union. Reprinted by arrangement with The Permissions Company, LLC on behalf of Shambhala Publications Inc., Boulder, CO, shambhala.com; **U6:** Project Gutenberg. (n.d.). Retrieved February 21, 2016, from www.gutenberg.org; **U8:** Consonant chart taken from *Cambridge International Dictionary of English*. Copyright © 1995 Cambridge University Press. Reproduced with kind permission of Cambridge University Press via PLSclear; **U15:** Polish language presentation and translation by Monika Grządka. Reproduced with kind permission; **U33:** Cambridge University Press for the text from 'Nurturing the relationships in our classrooms' by Sarah Mercer. Copyright © 2020 Cambridge University Press. Reproduced with kind permission; **U36** Council of Europe for the adapted text from 'A Common European Framework of Reference for Languages: Learning, Teaching, Assessment – Companion volume'. Copyright © 2020 Council of Europe. Reproduced with kind permission; **TM – U36:** Council of Europe for the adapted text from 'A Common European Framework of Reference for Languages: Learning, Teaching, Assessment – Companion volume'. Copyright © 2020 Council of Europe. Reproduced with kind permission.

Photography

The following photos are sourced from Getty Images:

TB – U13: funnybank/DigitalVision Vectors; Caiaimage/Chris Ryan; **U17:** arh-sib@rambler.ru/iStock Editorial/Getty Images Plus; Hans-Peter Merten/Photodisc; Tue Nguyen/EyeEm; Fergus O'Brien/The Image Bank/Getty Images Plus; Steve Allen/Stockbyte; Fotosearch; James D. Morgan/Getty Images News; **U20:** Jim Vecchion/Photo library; Harold M. Lambert/Archive Photos; **U21:** Spiderplay/E+; Siri Stafford/Photodisc; pop_jop/DigitalVision Vectors; **U23:** Jose Fuste Raga/Corbis; **U25:** Jane_Kelly/iStock/Getty Images Plus; MicrovOne/iStock/Getty Images Plus; **U36:** Juanmonino/E+; ajr_images/iStock/Getty Images Plus; **U37:** ShutterWorx/E+; Juanmonino/E+; **TM – U13:** filadendron/E+.

The following photos are sourced from another libraries:

TB – U5: imageBROKER/Alamy; **U21:** Superstock; **U36:** Steven May/Alamy.

TB – U21: Commissioned photography by Trevor Clifford.

Illustrations

TB – U8: Felicity House; Johanna Boccardo; Pat Murray; Tony Wilkins.

Typeset

Typesetting by QBS Learning.

Corpus

Development of this publication has made use of the Cambridge English Corpus(CEC). The CEC is a computer database of contemporary spoken and written English, which currently stands at over one billion words. It includes British English, American English and other varieties of English. It also includes the Cambridge Learner Corpus, developed in collaboration with the University of Cambridge ESOL Examinations. Cambridge University Press has built up the CEC to provide evidence about language use that helps us to produce better language teaching materials.